TEMARI
ADVENTURES
Fun & Easy Japanese Thread & Quilt Balls

DIANA VANDERVOORT

JAPAN PUBLICATIONS TRADING COMPANY

Published by JAPAN PUBLICATIONS TRADING CO., LTD.,
1-2-1 Sarugaku-cho, Chiyoda-ku, Tokyo, 101-0064 Japan

First edition, First printing: September 1998

Distributors:

UNITED STATES: *Kodansha America, Inc., through Oxford University Press,*
    198 Madison Avenue, New York, NY 10016.
CANADA: *Fitzhenry & Whiteside Ltd., 195 Allstate Parkway, Markham,*
    Ontario L3R 4T8.
UNITED KINGDOM and EUROPE: *Premier Book Marketing Ltd.,*
    1 Gower Street, London WC1E 6HA, England.
AUSTRALIA and NEW ZEALAND: *Bookwise International, 54 Crittenden Road,*
    Findon, South Australia 5023, Australia.
THE FAR EAST and JAPAN: *Japan Publications Trading Co., Ltd.,*
    1-2-1 Sarugaku-cho, Chiyoda-ku, Tokyo, 101-0064 Japan.

10 9 8 7 6 5 4 3 2 1

ISBN 4-88996-038-4

Printed in Japan

DEDICATION

This book is dedicated to "The Temari Girls," an extraordinary group of ladies, each one a veteran stitcher in her own right. We've met monthly for four years. They patiently allow me to try out my latest patterns, ideas and inventions, and give me invaluable feedback, alternative solutions, innovative suggestions, and giggle - a lot!

To you, Sherry Adkins, Carol Camerano, Vibs Claussen, Sharon McDuffy, Jamie Plockmeyer, Jennie Tanaka, and Riccamae Williams (who brings to each meeting her latest masterpiece biscotti recipe - each bettter than the last), with fondest friendship and sincerest thanks.

And to Taeko Hoffman, my cherished mentor and guide who keeps me on the correct pathways through my wonderings and wanderings amidst Japanese traditions, symbolism and motifs.

CONTENTS

List of COLOR ILLUSTRATIONS

from top: Christmas Fire (p.72), Window Ball with Appliqué (p.62)

from top: Simplified Kiku Snowflake Pattern (p.109), Double 8ths Offset Ball (p.104)

from top: Royal Renaissance (p.75), Snowflakes (p.114)

from top: Pentagons Basketweave (p.36), Halo Stars (p.123)

from top: Rings on Quiet Water (p.126), Quilt Quarters (p.94)

from top: Big Diamonds Obi (p.50), "Antiquity" ASANO-HA (p.79)

from top: Starshine (p.31), Petals (p.86)

from Top: Six Squares (p.100), Three Direction Wrapped Ball (p.40)

INTRODUCTION

This is a Beginner Book. You can enjoy these projects if you've never seen a temari before or if you are a veteran. I offer these ideas with the solitary motive of sharing with you the most wonderful craft I've ever known!

Temari is as unique as any needle art can be. It exists because it works! Its 1000-year traditions are well-grounded in simple methods that are practical, functional and proven. I was recently told of a young innovative teacher who uses temari in her classroom to teach the basic applications of geometry to her junior high school students.

Temari's popularity grows and grows because of its ability to solve problems with easy solutions and because of its intriguing ability to absorb the crafter with its developing designs. With curiosity and fascination, we explore the time-honored techniques that continue, time and again, to surprise and delight us with their flair and elegant simplicity of execution. Unlike anything else, its fascinations, its soothing serenities, its creative expansiveness, set temari apart from all other fiber art and craft forms.

As we explore, we find that the ancient methods of many craftspeople have left their touch on temari techniques. Hand-weavers, basket-weavers, fish-net makers, seamstresses, quilt-makers and embroiderers and makers of fine braids and ornamental wrapped surfaces of such things as sword handles and items of apparel, all become apparent in the different patterns.

Would you like some really *different* design ideas for Christmas gift ornaments, craft bazaars and home decorating accessories ?

Temari Adventures: Fun and Easy Japanese Thread and Quilt Balls assembles a collection of design ideas from a source that is historic and virtually unexplored by Western crafters. Number four in the series, this book reveals more of the ancient traditional patterns and combines them with simplified variations, many that can be finished in an evening.

Ribbon balls have wide ribbons substituted for individual threads, applied on surfaces wrapped with shiny metallic machine embroidery threads and embellished with brilliants pinned to the balls.

The Pentagon Basketweave reveals its probable origins from a toy ball woven from 6 strips of rattan, made in a moment by Grandfather Basketweaver for the delight of a child. An idea you'll use again and again, it's so simple. Its pattern can be applied in just minutes!

For some **thread balls,** narrow braided ribbon is substituted for the single thread applications, speeding the process to a fraction of time.

Quilt balls fascinated me from the moment I saw them. Fabric covered balls continue the tradition of recycled materials reborn into new life. I found that the special vividly colored kimonos of the Japanese Girls Day celebration commonly use temari as a motif. Fabric samples pictured balls that appeared to have fabrics, printed or embroidered, pieced and layered onto the balls. The fabrics seemed to be cut and pieced to utilize the printed or woven designs in the fabrics and eliminated or minimized the need for further detail or stitched embellishment. So I tried it!

Quilters! These are laden with possibilities! This is a method that will be extended into limitless inventions. Coordinate those colors and fabrics as you do so well! (I know those scraps are there). And display these along with your masterpiece hanging quilt for a focal point in room that will send them reeling!

Enjoy and Explore! Temari is a craft of invention.

GLOSSARY OF MATERIALS

All of the materials selected for use in this book have been chosen for their accessibility. In some cases brand names have been suggested in order to more specifically describe a material. In the case of the Pearl Cotton #5, DMC has been named exclusively for the projects in this book, however other brands such as Anchor will perform equally. For all of the materials listed, a generic description is provided for clarification, as well as the type of shop where the material can be purchased.

Styrofoam Balls - found in hobby or craft stores, the measurement size refers to the diameter of the ball, i.e. a 3 inch ball measures 3 inches through the center of the ball, not around the outside of the ball. Check each Styrofoam blank carefully before you buy for dents or flat spots on the surface; these make dividing the ball difficult.

Polyester Batting - also called Fleece-found in fabric stores, is 1/4 to 3/8 inch or 1/2 to 1 centimeter thick. It is commonly used for trapunto and appliqué, has low loft with consistent texture and thickness throughout. Batting can be purchased by the yard from a bolt or pre-cut in a plastic bag.

The Yarn Wrap - look in your craft store for spools of mini punch needle yarns, some are called "Purrfect Punch;" a wide range of colors are available. Baby, sock or sport weight yarn of consistent texture works well. Finer, light-weight yarns are preferable. Heavier weight yarns create lumps on the ball's surface. The yarn's color should be a similar color to the outer thread wrap.

The Thread Wrap - regular sewing thread, polyester or cotton, is the outer thread wrap. Select your Pearl Cotton #5 decorative threads first, then match the sewing thread to them. 200 yards cover a 3 inch ball (a medium spool or two small spools). A 4 inch ball takes one large spool, or a medium spool plus a small spool. For Metallics, see Madeira, Sulky of America and Y.L.I. Corporation below in this list.

Needles - temari requires a long sharp needle with a large eye. Cotton or Yarn Darners (2 1/2 inches long), size #18, may be found in fabric and needlecraft stores. One yarn tapestry needle is helpful in your pincushion.
   Fabric balls use Milliner's needles - medium long length and sharp.

Colored Glass-headed Pins should be 1 to 1 1/4 inches in length. A variety of 6 to 8 colors is helpful; purchased in fabric stores.

Dressmakers or straight pins are used for the petals ball and for attaching jewel embellishments through the fabric. Use longer length stainless steel pins with polished heads for refined appearance. Do not use beading pins, they are not long enough to secure through fabric.

Red Tomato Pin Cushion - to hold glass-headed pins separated by color.

Fabric Shears - for cutting polyester batting for balls and fabric pieces, the sharper the better.

Thread Scissors - small needlework scissors with sharp points for cutting single threads.

Centimeter Tape Measure - the common wind-up variety that measures 150 centimeters on one side of the tape and 60 inches on the backside. The narrower the better.

Measuring Papers - the best paper is copier paper (20 pound bond) cut on a paper cutter. 8 1/2 by 11 inch paper measures a 3 inch ball, legal size, 8 1/2 by 14 inch paper, measures a 4 inch ball. Cut paper strips lengthwise, 3/8 inch wide. Rice paper was probably used in Japan.

Paper and plastic bags for patterns - Circular Paper Patterns are used for templates on the Window Ball. Use any copier weight paper - 20 pound bond. Petal-shaped patterns cut from paper are used for the Petals Ball. Clear plastic produce bags from the grocery store work great for patterns for quilt balls. Put the ball inside. Smooth bag over ball. Draw around the mark lines with a "Sharpie" indelible marking pen. Cut out the pattern from the bag. See instructions in chapter.

Gold and Silver Metallic Marking Thread - generically called "knitting metallics" or "needlepoint/stitchery metallics." They can be found in needlecraft stores, larger yarn and craft shops. They should be 6 to 10 strands, twisted or braided, not chained or wrapped. Kreinik's Balger Ombre, Japan Braid, Cord and Ribbon produce excellent results. Colors and variety are exceptional. Kreinik Mfg. Co., P. O. Box 1966, Parkersburg, WV 26101.
　　　Also try "Candlelight" by YLI Corp., see below.

Surface Decoration Threads - Pearl Cotton #5 weight. DMC and Anchor are commonly accessible, have a huge variety of hues and shades and provide ease in keying colors and shades. Two skeins approximately equal one ball. Prepare skeined threads by wrapping around a cardboard card 2 by 3 inches. Write the color number and manufacturer on the card for future reference.

"Watercolors" by Caron Collection are handpainted (overdyed) cottons, 3 plies of #5 weight when separated. "Waterlilies" is 12 strand hand-painted silk. Caron Collection, 67 Poland St., Bridgeport, CN 06605.

Rainbow Gallery produces a huge variety of novelty threads and woven braids and ribbons for stitchery. Look in your needle craft shop for "Fyre Werks" ® Hologram and Metallic Ribbons and Neon Rays ® which are woven 1/16 inch rayon ribbon. Rainbow Gallery, 7412 Fulton Ave. #5, N. Hollywood, CA 91605.

Rhode Island Textiles produces "RibbonFloss" ™ and metallic "RibbonFloss" ™ is flat-woven, about 1/16 inch wide in a beautiful range of colors, and "Reflections" ™ RibbonFloss™ has a formal glossy look and a pliable quality that is easy to work. Ask your local needlecraft shop or Rhode Island Textile Co., P. O. Box 999, Pawtucket, RI 02862, or Nancy's Notions - Beaver Dam, WI (414) 887-0391.

Y. L. I. "Candlelight" metallics are perfect for marking thread, come in a wonderful variety of colors on 75 yard spools and can be commonly found in larger needlecraft stores. Y. L. I. also has a collection of Bunka threads and silk twisted thread color-keyed to match the silk ribbons, and machine embroidery threads in many colors on spools in your local fabric store. YLI Corporation, 161 West Main Street, Rock Hill, SC 29730, (803) 985-3100.

Madeira Threads have a vast array of 6-strand cotton floss and metallics in pull-out packages, and a tremendous variety of machine embroidery metallics on spools including hologram metallics in several colors called "Jewel". Look for them in fabric stores. Contact S.C.S. U.S.A., 9631 Northeast Colfax St., Portland, OR 97220-1232.

Sulky of America produces machine embroidery thread of high twinkle. "Sliver Metallic" comes in several colors and is found at your fabric store. Sulky of America, 3113 Broadpoint Dr., Harbor Heights, FL 33983.

Mill Hill-Gay Bowles Sales, Inc. produces the finest quality beads and jewel-like embellishments called "Glass Treasures" and "Crystal Treasures." Ask your local needlecraft shop. Gay Bowles Sales, Inc., P. O. Box 1060, Janesville, WI, (608) 754-9466.

Ribbons for ribbon balls - look in the ribbons and trims and bridal departments of your fabric store and the floral department of craft stores for fabric ribbons. Wire Ribbon doesn't work. Widths are listed according to size of the ball: 3-inch ball - choose ribbon no wider than 5/8 inch; 4-inch ball - ribbon no wider than 3/4 inch. Go narrower instead of wider when selecting.

Fabrics for Quilt balls - lighter weight cottons, silks, rayons and synthetics work best. For Gold and metallic lame', use "tissue" lame' rather than "liquid." Men's ties work great - look in your thrift store. The Japanese prints used here are cotton from "Q" is for Quilts, 620 South Glenoaks, Burbank, CA 91502, (818) 567-0267.

Azabu-ya has the authentic silks of profoundly exquisite quality and colors. Mariko is happy to assist with selection of color combinations and has pre-packaged selections that are combined for you. Azabu-ya Japanese Quilt Shop, 1953 Westwood Blvd., Los Angeles, CA 90025, (310) 446-1831.

Other Materials To Try:

"Bunka" Japanese Rayon Chainette made by KAO Brand (color numbers used are from KAO Brand Bunka color card). When unchained or pulled out it produces a finer gauge, non-stretch, crepe-like texture. In its pulled out state, it is called "Rydian." It has a beautiful range of very typical Japanese colors, keyed for combinations, from the vivid brilliants to the subtle neutrals (called "Shibui"). Dampen it slightly to remove the kinks. A favorite temari material in Japan - but watch out, it fades. Order from "LACIS" 3163 Adeline St., Berkeley, CA 94703.

Brazilian Embroidery Threads can be used for stitched patterns only. Because they are rayon, they are too slick for wrapped designs. They provide a beautiful array of colors and a very formal, polished, silky sheen. Order from Edmar Co., P. O. Box 55, Camarillo, CA 93011.

Needle Necessities has overdyed and shadow-dyed fibers of all types in exquisite colors. 14746 N. E. 95th St. Redmond, WA 98052.

For mail order information and special assistance on threads, color cards, and other temari materials, WEAVER'S NEEDLE and FRAME - 2130-C Newbury Road, Newbury Park, CA 91320, phone (805) 499-7979, fax (805) 499-1059.

GLOSSARY OF SYMBOLS

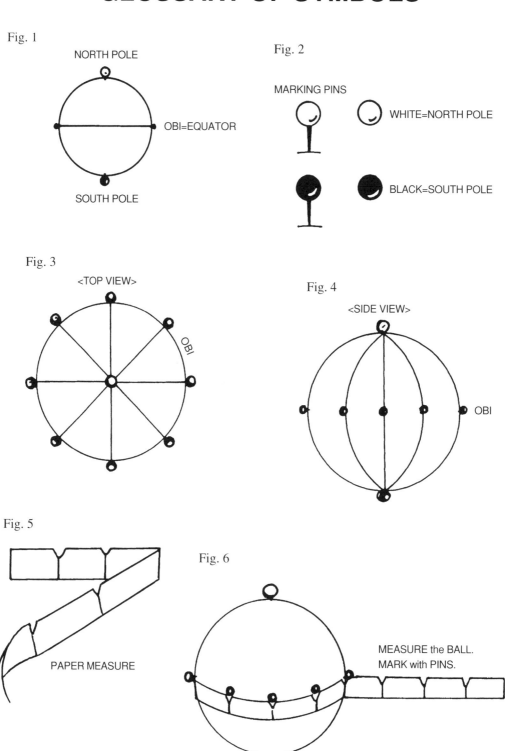

Fig. 1

NORTH POLE

OBI=EQUATOR

SOUTH POLE

Fig. 2

MARKING PINS

WHITE=NORTH POLE

BLACK=SOUTH POLE

Fig. 3

<TOP VIEW>

OBI

Fig. 4

<SIDE VIEW>

OBI

Fig. 5

PAPER MEASURE

Fig. 6

MEASURE the BALL.
MARK with PINS.

Fig. 7

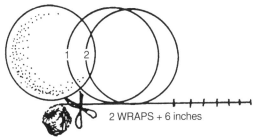
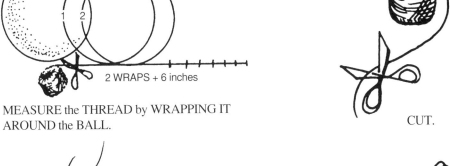

2 WRAPS + 6 inches

MEASURE the THREAD by WRAPPING IT
AROUND the BALL.

Fig. 8

CUT.

Fig. 9

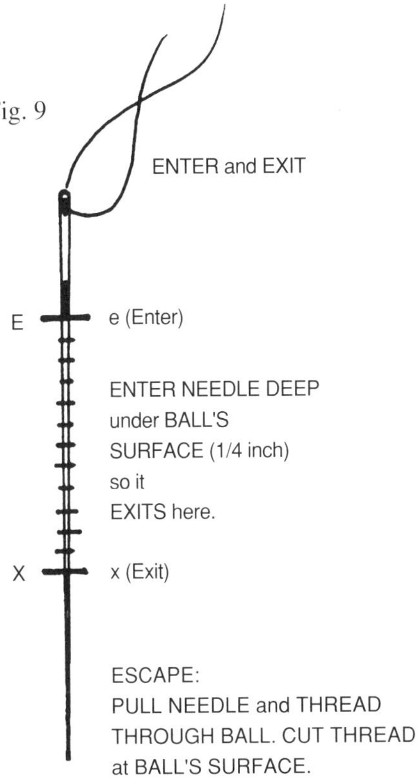

ENTER and EXIT

E   e (Enter)

ENTER NEEDLE DEEP
under BALL'S
SURFACE (1/4 inch)
so it
EXITS here.

X   x (Exit)

ESCAPE:
PULL NEEDLE and THREAD
THROUGH BALL. CUT THREAD
at BALL'S SURFACE.

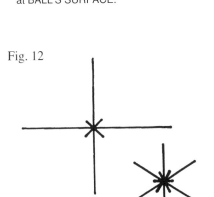

Fig. 10

WRAP or PROCEED in DIRECTION
of the ARROWS.

Fig. 11

USE PINS to ALIGN THREADS.

PIVOT THREADS around the PIN.

Fig. 12

TACK INTERSECTIONS of MARK THREADS.

Fig. 13

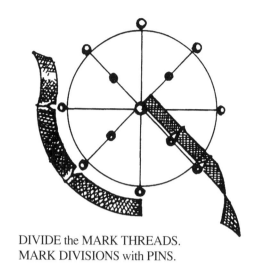

DIVIDE the MARK THREADS.
MARK DIVISIONS with PINS.

Fig. 14

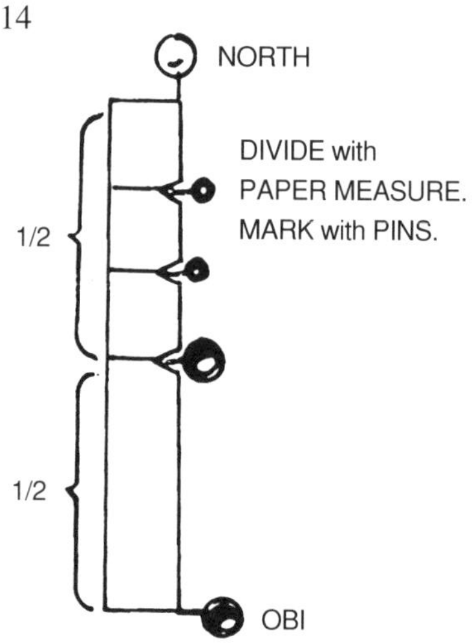

NORTH

DIVIDE with
PAPER MEASURE.
MARK with PINS.

1/2

1/2

OBI

Fig. 15

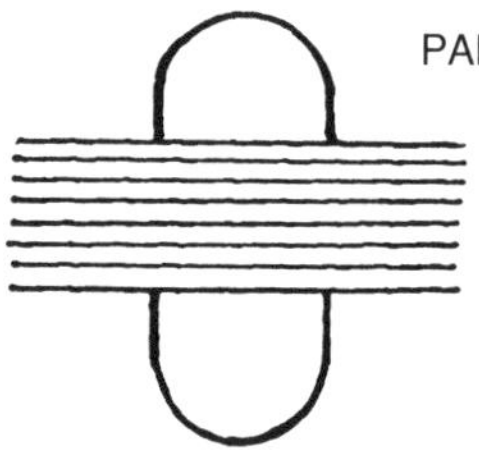

PAPER TAB

SLIDE PAPER TAB under PATTERN
THREADS.
PUSH NEEDLE, EYE-END FIRST,
between TAB and THREADS.

Fig. 17

THREAD NEEDLE

DO NOT CUT THREAD
from BALL.

Fig. 16

KEEPER PINS

INSERT SIDE by SIDE,
CLOSE TOGETHER, at OBI LINE.

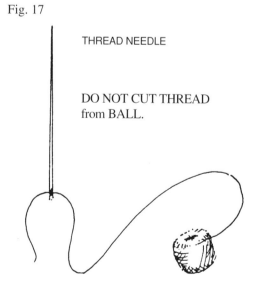

Fig. 18

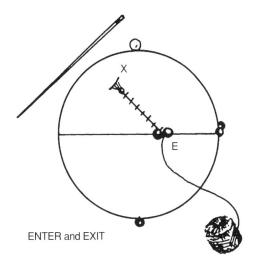

ENTER and EXIT

REMOVE NEEDLE from THREAD.
PULL THREAD'S END under BALL'S
SURFACE.

Fig. 19

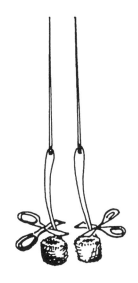

THREAD 2 NEEDLES
with 2 COLORS
to ALTERNATE QUICKLY.

The Division Symbols

DIVIDE and MARK the BALL into:

Fig. 20

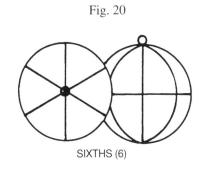

SIXTHS (6)

Fig. 21

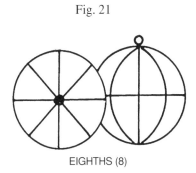

EIGHTHS (8)

Fig. 22

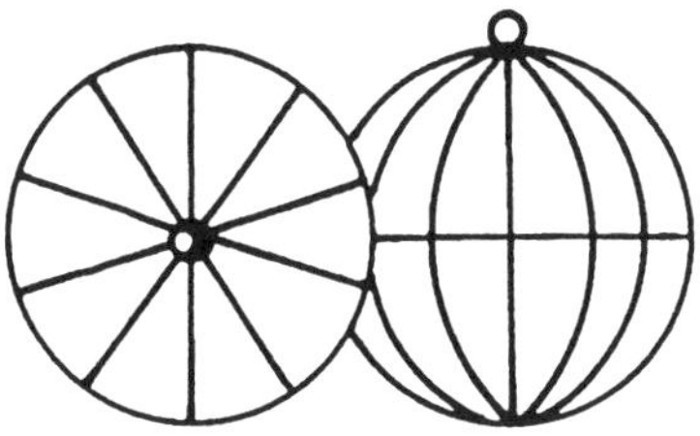

TENTHS (10)

Fig. 23

DOUBLE EIGHTHS

Fig. 24

PENTAGONS

WRAP THE BALL

METHOD: THE BATTING LAYER

Fig. 1

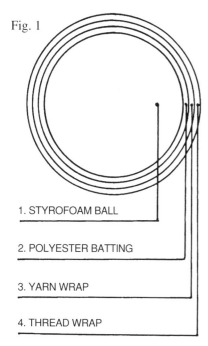

1. STYROFOAM BALL

2. POLYESTER BATTING

3. YARN WRAP

4. THREAD WRAP

CUT 2 RECTANGLES OF BATTING.

Fig. 2

for 3 inch ball

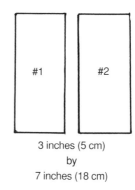

3 inches (5 cm)
by
7 inches (18 cm)

Fig. 3

for 4 inch ball

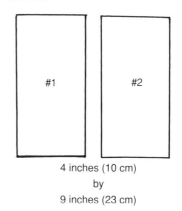

4 inches (10 cm)
by
9 inches (23 cm)

Fig. 4

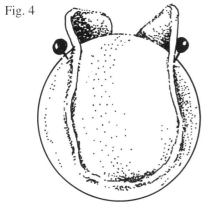

Lay on batting
Rectangle #1.
PIN ENDS to ball.

Fig. 5

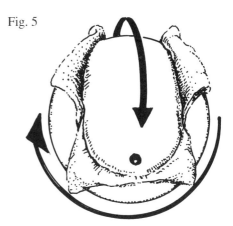

Lay on batting
Rectangle #2 crosswise.
PIN ENDS to ball.

Fig. 6

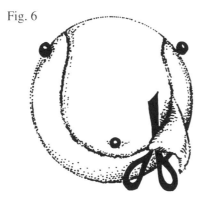

TRIM off corners
and excess to fit
precisely.

RANDOM WRAP THE YARN LAYER.
REMOVE THE PINS.

Fig. 7

RANDOM WRAP
THE THREAD LAYER.

Fig. 8

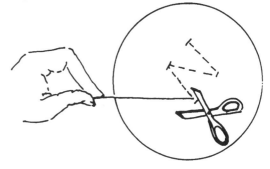

TO FINISH:
THREAD END into NEEDLE.
STITCH into BALL.
CUT at BALL'S SURFACE.

DIVIDE THE BALL

THE NORTH POLE

PAPER MEASURE:
Fold 1/4 inch from end. Pin fold.

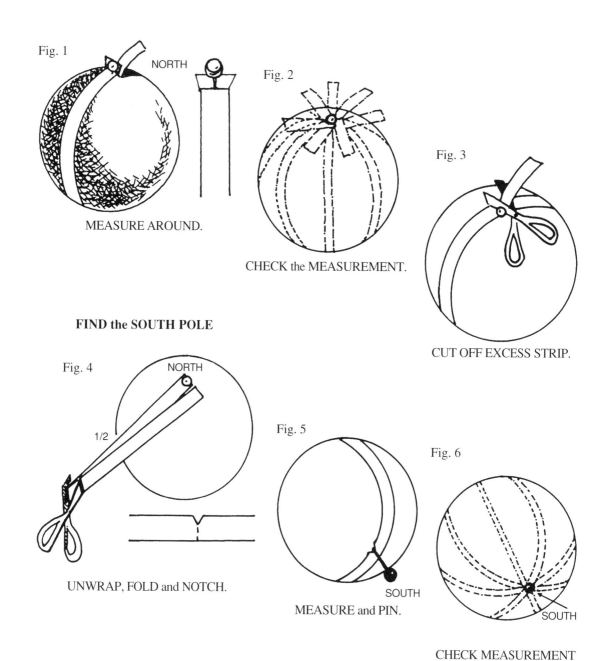

Fig. 1

NORTH

MEASURE AROUND.

Fig. 2

CHECK the MEASUREMENT.

Fig. 3

CUT OFF EXCESS STRIP.

FIND the SOUTH POLE

Fig. 4

NORTH

1/2

UNWRAP, FOLD and NOTCH.

Fig. 5

SOUTH

MEASURE and PIN.

Fig. 6

SOUTH

CHECK MEASUREMENT
and CENTER the PIN.

FIND THE OBI LINE

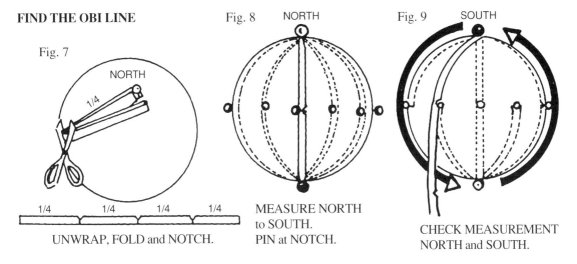

Fig. 7

NORTH

1/4

| 1/4 | 1/4 | 1/4 | 1/4 |

UNWRAP, FOLD and NOTCH.

Fig. 8   NORTH

MEASURE NORTH
to SOUTH.
PIN at NOTCH.

Fig. 9   SOUTH

CHECK MEASUREMENT
NORTH and SOUTH.

TO FIND 8 DIVISIONS AROUND THE OBI LINE

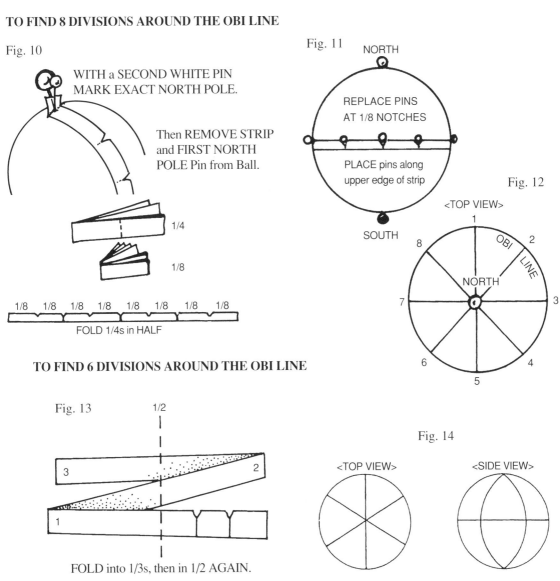

Fig. 10

WITH a SECOND WHITE PIN
MARK EXACT NORTH POLE.

Then REMOVE STRIP
and FIRST NORTH
POLE Pin from Ball.

1/4

1/8

| 1/8 | 1/8 | 1/8 | 1/8 | 1/8 | 1/8 | 1/8 | 1/8 |

FOLD 1/4s in HALF

Fig. 11   NORTH

REPLACE PINS
AT 1/8 NOTCHES

PLACE pins along
upper edge of strip

SOUTH

Fig. 12

<TOP VIEW>

OBI LINE

NORTH

TO FIND 6 DIVISIONS AROUND THE OBI LINE

Fig. 13   1/2

3   2

1

FOLD into 1/3s, then in 1/2 AGAIN.

Fig. 14

<TOP VIEW>   <SIDE VIEW>

27

MARK THE BALL

METHOD: FOR 8 DIVISIONS

Fig. 1

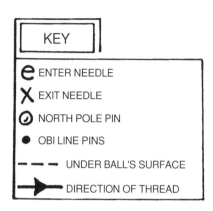

Fig. 2

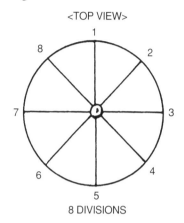

<TOP VIEW>

8 DIVISIONS

Fig. 3

Fig. 4

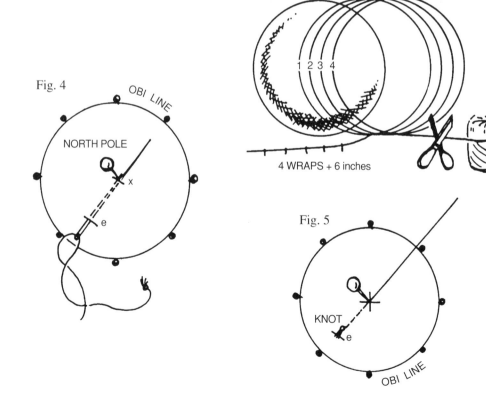

MEASURE MARKING THREAD

4 WRAPS + 6 inches

Fig. 5

PULL THREAD END UNDER SURFACE.

Fig. 6

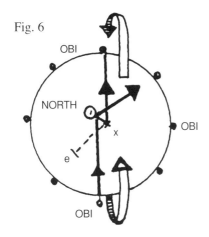

WRAP THREAD AROUND BALL.

Fig. 7

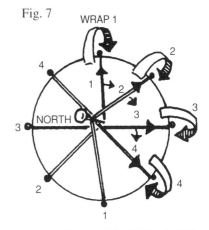

USE NORTH, SOUTH and OBI
MARK PINS to ALIGN
THREAD WRAPS.

Fig. 8

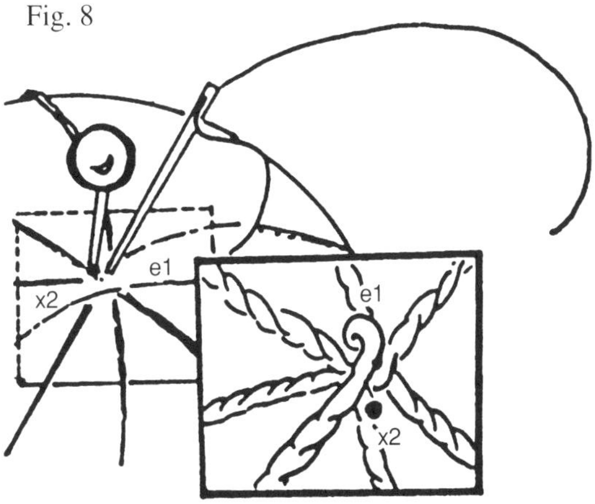

Fig. 9

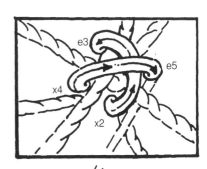

TACK INTERSECTIONS
at NORTH and SOUTH
POLE PINS.

ESCAPE

Fig. 10

TACK

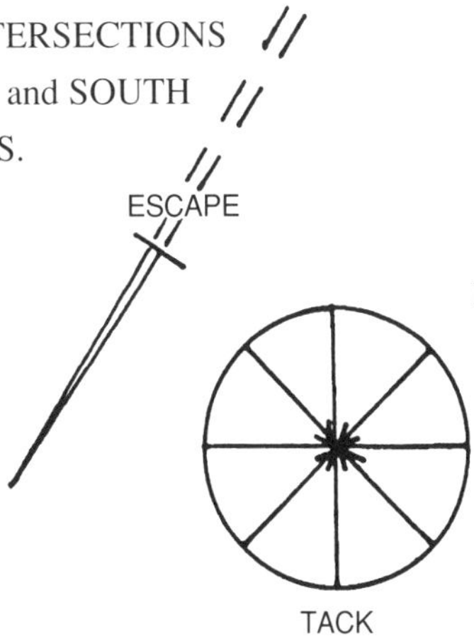

Fig. 11

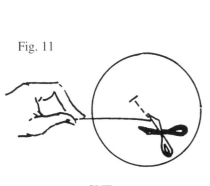

CUT.

MARKING THE OBI LINE

Fig. 12

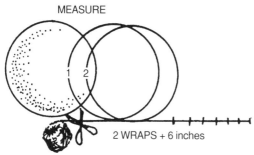

MEASURE

2 WRAPS + 6 inches

Fig. 13

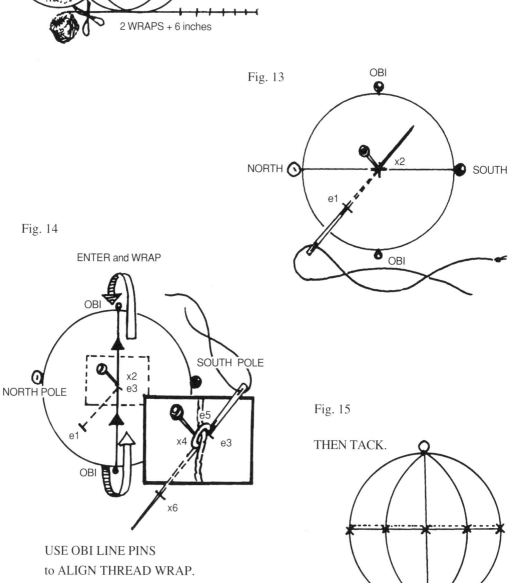

OBI

NORTH   x2   SOUTH

e1

OBI

Fig. 14

ENTER and WRAP

OBI

NORTH POLE

x2
e3

e1

SOUTH POLE

e5

x4   e3

x6

USE OBI LINE PINS
to ALIGN THREAD WRAP.

Fig. 15

THEN TACK.

Ball #1
Ribbon Ball   "**Starshine**"

These patterns have been designed specifically as Quick and Easy versions of Temari thread balls. Very fast and time efficient, they are made using 3 inch Styrofoam balls that are wrapped in the conventional way with sewing thread that is later combined with metallic embroidery thread for extra surface sparkle.

Simple divisions have 1/4 to 5/8 inch wide ribbons applied over mark lines. Bright and shiny ribbons and braids can be found in fabric stores. Check the Bridal Department for glittery golds and silvers, the Notions and Trims Department for colored metallic and grosgrain ribbons.

These balls are further embellished with beads and spangles. Mill Hill's Antique Glass beads, "Crystal Treasures" and "Glass Treasures" are used here. Look for them in your Stitchery Shop.

Both the ribbons and embellishments are pinned to the balls — it doesn't get much faster than that!

MEASURING THE AMOUNT OF RIBBON
Every ball has a slightly different measurement. Here, 3 inch balls are used. Measure the correct amount of ribbon on a wrapped ball. Measure the circumference (1 wrap) plus 1 1/2 inches extra. The APPROXIMATE measurement for a 3 inch ball is 12 inches per strip. Always check YOUR measurements first so you don't come up short! I always buy a little extra to be sure.

MATERIALS:

3 inch Styrofoam ball — Christmas green thread wrap

YLI machine embroidery thread

3 Ribbons — 2 Very glittery metallic silver/gold combinations that coordinate patterns

>   3/8 inch wide — 1 1/2 yards = 4 strips approximately 12 inches each — 3 strips go North to South plus 1 Strip around Obi (48 inches)

>   1/8 inch wide — 2 1/2 yards = 6 strips North to South. (72 inches)

>   5/8 inch wide Red Satin — 1/2 yard — 1 strip at Obi (12 inches)

Straight pins (dressmaker)

Scissors

Paper strip

Extra sewing thread — Contrasting color

Needle — Yarn Darner #18

Embellishments:
Mill Hill's "Glass Treasures" Snowflakes —
>   2 Large Gold #12040
>   6 Small Gold #12038
>   6 Small Silver #12037

METHOD:

Wrap the ball in the regular way - batting, then yarn wrap.
Then apply a thin thread wrap.
When the thread color covers the yarn, combine the metallic embroidery thread and wrap the 2 spools on together.
Without the sewing thread, the metallic itself is too slick to adhere to the ball. (Don't try this at home).
Wrap a liberal cover of the 2 threads combined.
Additional metallic may be wrapped over the surface after but be prepared to stitch large zig zag stitches over the surface with regular sewing thread to make sure threads stay in place.

DIVIDE the ball into 6ths:

First find the North and South Poles.
With 1/2s and 1/4s on your paper measure, locate the Obi Line. (Figure 1)

Fig. 1
LOCATE

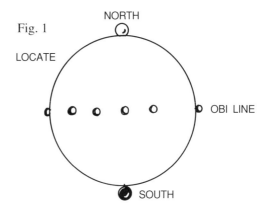

Fig. 2

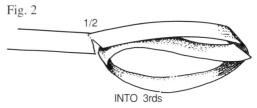

INTO 3rds

Fig. 3

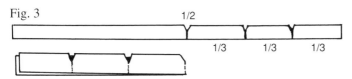

Fig. 4

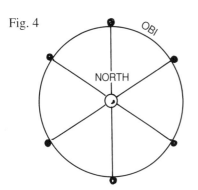

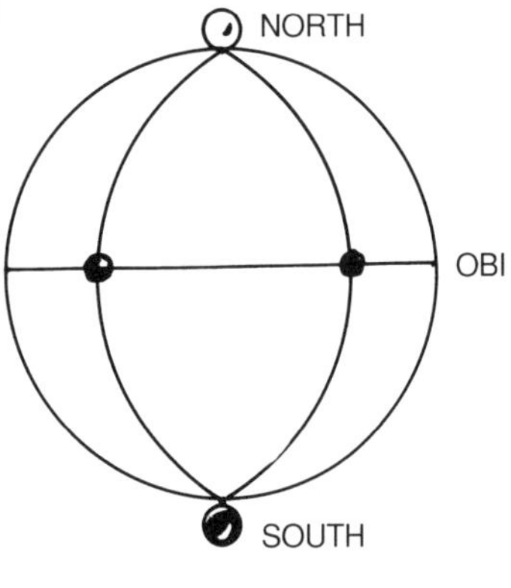

To divide into 6ths around the Obi Line, divide 1/2 the paper (North to South measurement) into 3rds. Do this by making a loop in 1/2 the paper and adjust the loop until 3rds are equal. Notch the 1/3 folds. (Figure 2)

Fold the paper at the 1/2 Mark (South Pole) and place 1/3 Marks onto the second 1/2 by folding the paper together at the 1/3 Mark notches. (Figure 3)

Keep all notches on the same side.

Place the paper around the Obi. Place Pins at the 1/6 Mark notches. (Figure 4)

MARK the divisions with sewing thread in a contrasting color. (Figure 5)

TACK the North and South Poles and Obi line intersections. The Mark Lines are your guides for even placement of ribbons on the ball. This is what makes it a snap!

Fig. 6

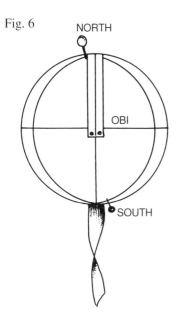

NORTH

OBI

SOUTH

MEASURE and CUT 3 strips of 3/8 inch Ribbon.
— 1 Wrap plus 1 and 1/2 inches each.

Be sure to turn strips so the pattern in the
ribbon all goes the same direction.

BEGIN at the OBI LINE. Apply strip #1 so
one end overlaps 1/2 inch below the Obi Line,
the long length goes over the North Pole.
PIN with 2 straight pins 1/4 inch from the end
of the strip. (Figure 6)

Use a mark line over the North Pole and follow
it centering the strip.
Remove the North Pole pin and place it
at the side of the intersection.
Continue the ribbon over the North Pole,
around the South Pole and back to the start.

Pull the ribbon taut onto the ball.
Pin with 2 straight pins about 1/4 inch above
the Obi Line. Ends will overlap. Extra is
cut off to 1/2 inch so Obi wrap will cover all
starts and ends. Trim the 3 ends before
beginning the 1/8 inch wraps. (Figure 7)

Fig. 7

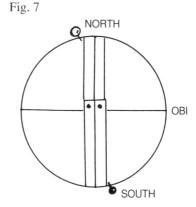

NORTH

OBI

SOUTH

Apply the 2 remaining 3/8 inch strips to the
North/South Mark Lines. (Figure 8)

THE 1/8 INCH Wide Ribbon STRIPS:

MEASURE and CUT 6 strips - 1 wrap plus
1 1/2 inches.
BEGIN at the OBI LINE.
The 1/8 inch ribbons are wrapped at a Diagonal
1/2 inch to the Right and Left of the North Pole
and South Pole. Continue in a straight line
around the ball.

Fig. 8

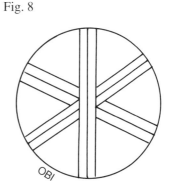

OBI

Fig. 9

Fig. 10

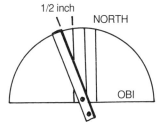

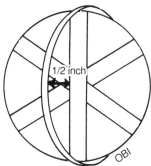

Begin by overlapping one end at the Obi Line
at a Diagonal. Pin with 2 pins at the correct angle.
Wrap to the Left, cross the Obi Line on the
opposite side. End where you began.
Pin with 2 pins. (Figures 9, 10)

Fig. 11

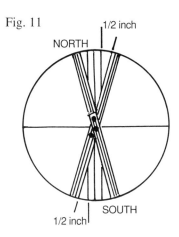

Wrap #2 on a Diagonal to the Right,
1/2 inch to the Right of the North and South.
Pin the end with 2 pins. Cut off the ends at
1/2 inch overlap. (Figure 11)

Fig. 12

Apply the 4 remaining 1/8 inch wide ribbons
to the 2 remaining North/South Mark Lines
1/2 inch out from the Poles. (Figure 12)

THE OBI LINE:

MEASURE and CUT the 5/8 inch wide
Red Satin Ribbon — 1 wrap plus 1 1/2 inches.

To begin, Pin with 2 pins 1/4 from the end.
Wrap the Red Satin Ribbon around the ball.
Pull taut onto the surface. Pin with 2 pins
at the overlap. (Figure 13)

Fig. 13

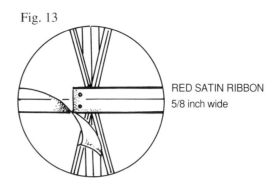

RED SATIN RIBBON
5/8 inch wide

Fig. 14

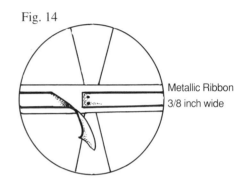

Metallic Ribbon
3/8 inch wide

Apply the final metallic 3/8 inch wide
Obi strip on top of the Red Satin Ribbon.
Plan the beginning so that the ending can be
doubled over at the edge of one of the 6 points.
(Figure 14)
Pin the beginning 1/4 inch from the edge with
2 pins. Pull the strip taut around the ball.

Fig. 15

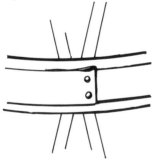

Fold the excess at the end so the fold edge lines
up along the edge of one point. Pin along the
fold edge. (Figure 15)

Embellish with Mill Hill's "Crystal Treasures"
Snowflakes.
Pin Medium Gold Snowflakes #12038 and
Medium Silver Snowflakes #12037 in pairs
in the triangle spaces above and below the
Obi Line. (Figure 16)

Fig. 16

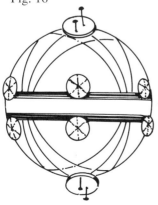

Pin 2 Large Gold Snowflakes #12040 at the
North and South Poles. Tack the Snowflakes
across their centers with sewing thread or
clear nylon thread to fasten securely to the ball.

Stitch on a hanging loop at the Obi Line with
needle and thread.

The ball is complete.

Ribbon Ball "Pentagons Basketweave"

This is a woven ribbon design you'll use again and again! From humble beginnings
as a toy ball made of rattan for child's play, its potential for design invention is endless.
There is no division mark applied to the ball. The design creates itself!

    This simplified version of the design is fabric ribbon applied over a ball that is wrapped
with a combination of sewing thread together with a matching color of metallic machine
embroidery thread so the thread wrap becomes part of the decorative surface.

    For a traditional fabric-covered ball, cover the thread wrap with circles of contrasting fabric.

MATERIALS:

3 inch Styrofoam ball, low loft batting 1/4 inch thick —
2 rectangles 3 inches by 7 inches
Very Lightweight yarn — color similar to sewing thread

Sewing Thread — Yellow Orange Medium spool 300
yards to match Sulky "Sliver Metallic" #145-8006

Metallic machine embroidery thread by Sulky

"Sliver Metallic" #145-8006 to match sewing thread

Dressmaker Pins

Needles — sharp long Milliner's Yarn Darner #18

Sewing thread — match the ribbon

Ribbon — decorative fabric trim

YOUR Wrapped BALL MAY BE LARGER OR
SMALLER THAN THE MEASUREMENTS GIVEN
for strips. PRE-MEASURE and CHECK
ALL MEASUREMENTS TO FIT YOUR BALL
BEFORE YOU CUT RIBBON STRIPS.

For 3 inch ball wrapped with batting, yarn, thread:
    6 STRIPS of ribbon or fabric with edges turned under
    WIDTH: NO WIDER THAN 5/8 INCH or 1.5 cm
    LENGTH: 1 WRAP PLUS 1 1/2 INCHES = about 12 inches each
    Total length needed — 2 yards

For 4 inch ball - 6 STRIPS
    WIDTH: NO WIDER THAN 3/4 INCH or 2 cm
    LENGTH: 1 WRAP PLUS 1 1/2 INCHES = 15 inches each
    Total length needed — 2 1/2 yards

Tips Ribbons wider than 5/8 inch for a wrapped 3-inch ball and 3/4 inch for a wrapped
4-inch ball will not lay flat on the ball at the corners. Go to a narrower width but no wider.
Buy an extra 1/2 yard of ribbon — just in case! Select Ribbons with a pronounced stripe.
Busy patterns can blur the design.

Optional: Contrasting colored fabric — 1/8 yard is used to cover the thread wrap if
metallic decorative thread wrap is not used. Circles of fabric are applied after ribbon is in place.

Fig. 1

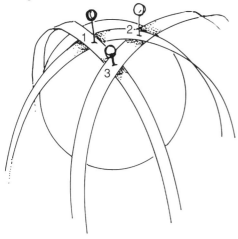

Preparation:

Apply batting to Styrofoam ball.

Random wrap with very lightweight yarn
— cover the white.

Random wrap with sewing thread.
Cover yarn with a thin layer then combine
metallic embroidery thread.
Wrap on the 2 together until the surface is
covered.
To end, thread both ends into the Yarn Darner
#18 needle. Then take several large Zig Zag
stitches all over the ball's surface to hold the
metallic in place as you work.

NO DIVIDING OR MARKING IS NEEDED.

A traditional fabric ball is covered all over with
fabric. Apply just a light coating of thread wrap
to smooth down any lumps in the yarn. Yarn
lumps make the fabric surface appear bumpy.

Fig. 2

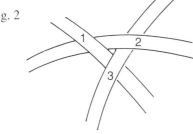

Fabric strips may be made — edges trimmed or
bound with another color of narrower ribbon.
Enhance the design by exaggerating the stripes.
2 layers of different widths of colored ribbon
may be machine stitched or glued before the
6 strips are cut.

CUT the Ribbon yardage into 6 equal strips, each
about 12 inches for a 3 inch wrapped ball.
Lay the 6 strips out together. Make sure any
pattern in the ribbon runs the same direction.

Fig. 3

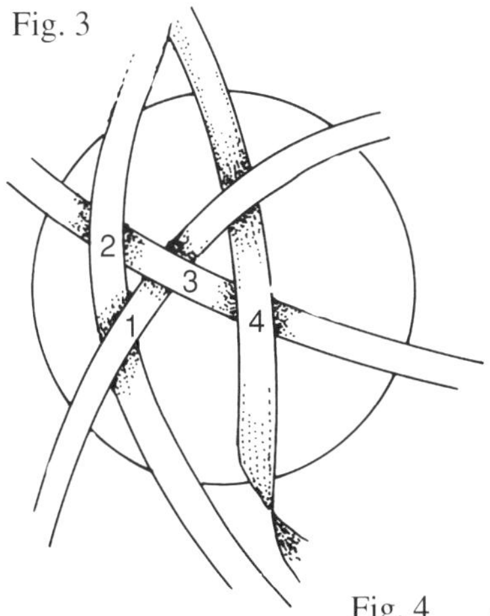

Lay 3 strips on the ball at their approximate CENTERS
and shape a TRIANGLE of EQUAL SIDES. At the corners
of the Triangle, the strips go over and under, Right Over
Left. (Figures 1, 2)

PIN IN PLACE tentatively — the ends are hanging down.

Fig. 4

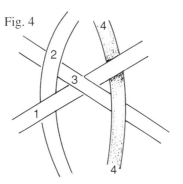

ADD STRIP #4 on the Right Side Corner:
An ADJOINING TRIANGLE is created.
Weave corners OVER and UNDER
— Right Over Left. Pin in place.
This now looks like "Batman's Mask."
(Figures 3, 4)

ADD STRIP #5 Below "Batman's Mask":
It closes the Pentagon at the bottom.
Keep Triangles evenly shaped and
weave corners Right Over Left.
Pin in place. (Figure 5)

Fig. 5

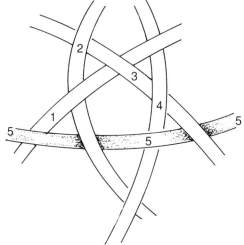

ADD STRIP #6:
INTERWEAVE. Strip #6 goes
approximately around the Obi Line.
Begin Strip #6 by starting its end
underneath an adjacent strip.
As it is woven, it completes the shapes
on the upper half of the ball,
picks up the ends of the other strips and
interweaves them. (Figure 6)

Fig. 6

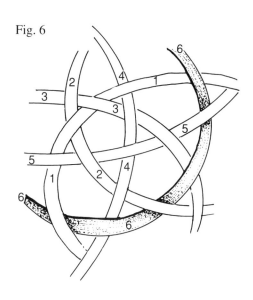

The remainder is interwoven to the bottom of
the ball. Work all around the ball, not just
one strip at a time.

Complete the weaving of the strips around the
bottom. Pin tentatively as you go.

FINISHING — DISGUISING THE ENDS:
When the weaving is completed,
ONE strip at a time is unpinned and the end
pulled backward under the nearest row and
pinned again underneath.
Pin near the end before you pull.
Repeat with all 6 strips. (Figure 7)

Fig. 7

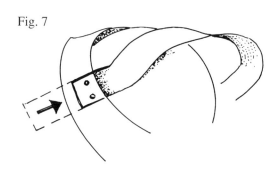

Fig. 8

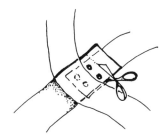

Make sure each strip fits tight onto the ball.
First pin with 2 pins the ends of ribbon layers
that go under other strips. Cut off extra overlap
that peeks out from underneath.
Then pin ends of strips that go over.
Push aside the overlapping strip,
Pin the 2 ends underneath. (Figure 8)
Then push the overlap strip back into place
over the top to hide the ends. (Figure 9)

ENDS MAY REMAIN PINNED if the thread
wrap is to show.

OR ENDS ARE STITCHED TOGETHER
ONTO THE BALL for the traditional
fabric-covered ball.

First stitch with thread the ends that go under
others. Cut off extra strip. Then stitch ends of
strips that go over. Stitch the strip ends together
making sure the strip fits tight onto the ball.
The overlapping strip may be pushed aside
while stitching the 2 ends together.
Then the overlap strip is pushed back into place
over the top to hide the ends.

Fig. 9

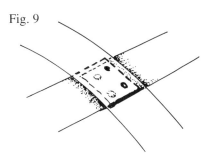

Fig. 10

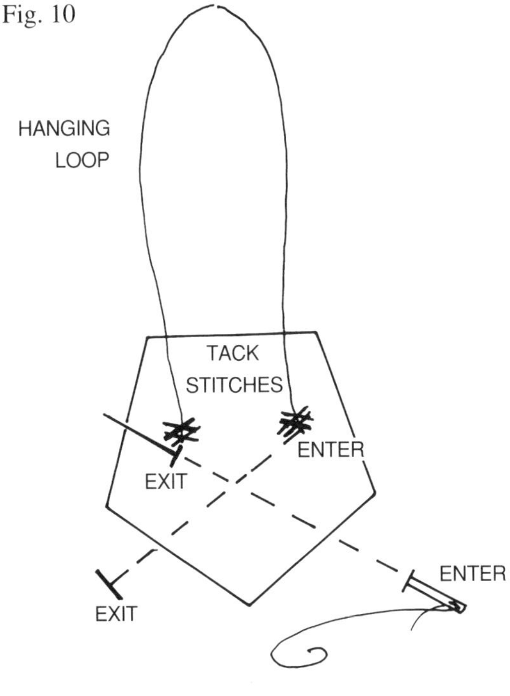

HANGING
LOOP

TACK
STITCHES

ENTER

EXIT

ENTER

EXIT

TO COVER the THREAD WRAP in
Pentagon Spaces:
    Cut 12 circles of contrasting fabric that
    measure the diameter of a pentagon plus
    1/2 inch seam allowance around the circle
    for Underlap. Slide the fabric circles
    under the strips, into the Center Spaces of
    the Pentagons. Use the eye-end of a needle
    to help with their placement. With needle
    and thread, Blind Stitch strips to inserted
    fabric circles.

With needle and thread, stitch on a hanging
loop.(Figure 10)

The ball is complete.

Three Direction Wrapped Ball

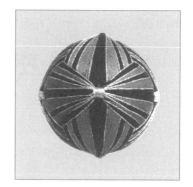

This ball works best with extreme light and dark contrast in the thread colors and the metallic. Dark or black thread wrap helps disguise the workings. Light pastel colors used together do not show the metallic directional lines.

Use the darkest color last for Direction Number 3. It is hard to avoid picking up a few surface threads with the final stitched wrap. If final color is similar to the thread wrap, these won't show.

MATERIALS:

2 inch ball — Black thread wrap

DMC Pearl Cotton #5 in 4 colors
  Black #310
  Orange #349
  Magenta #915
  Green #991

Metallic Gold — either Kreinik's Balger Ombre Gold #2000 or Y L I "Candlelight" Gold

Mark thread — Sewing thread in a contrasting color to Black Wrap

Fig. 1

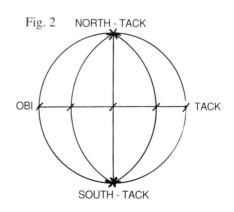

Eighths (8) Division

DIVIDE the ball into 8ths with an Obi. (Figure 1)

MARK the ball with the contrasting sewing thread. It will be completely covered by the pattern.

TACK the NORTH POLE, SOUTH POLE and OBI LINE INTERSECTIONS. (Figure 2)

Fig. 2   NORTH - TACK

OBI   TACK

SOUTH - TACK

Fig. 3

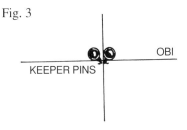

OBI

KEEPER PINS

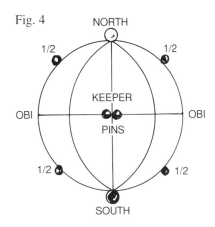

Fig. 4

NORTH

1/2   1/2

KEEPER

OBI   OBI

PINS

1/2   1/2

SOUTH

FIRST DIRECTIONAL WRAP:

On one 8th mark line, at the OBI Line,
place 2 KEEPER PINS SIDE BY SIDE.
On the same line, OPPOSITE SIDE of the ball,
place Keeper Pins at the Obi Line.
(Figures 3, 4)

Fig. 5

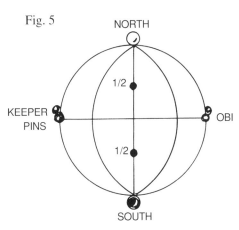

NORTH

1/2

KEEPER   OBI
PINS

1/2

SOUTH

From this 8th Mark line, TURN the ball 1/4
TURN. Use your 1/8 mark on your paper tape
to divide this line in 1/2 between the North Pole
and Obi and same line, South Pole and Obi.
Repeat on the same line, opposite side of
the ball. (Figure 5)

Fig. 6

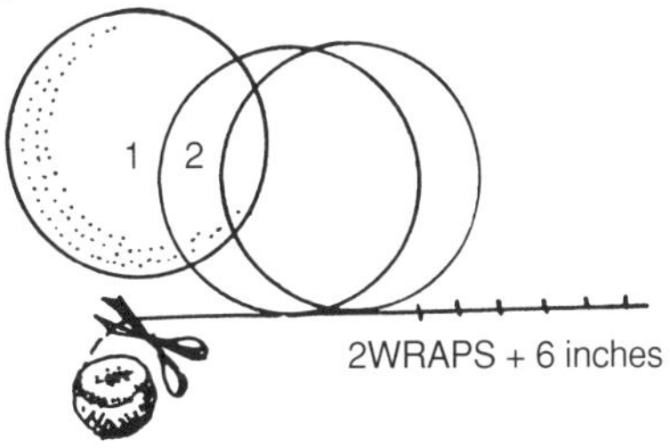

1   2

2WRAPS + 6 inches

FIRST ROWS — Metallic Gold.
MEASURE and Cut 2 WRAPS plus 6 inches of
Gold thread. Thread your needle,
KNOT the thread's end. (Figure 6)

ENTER the needle to EXIT IN BETWEEN
the Keeper Pins at the Obi Line.
Pull thread through so the knot disappears
under the ball's surface. (Figure 7)

Fig. 7

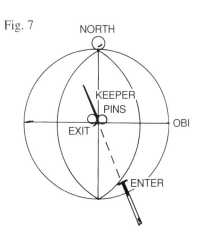

NORTH

KEEPER
PINS

OBI

EXIT

ENTER

41

Fig. 8

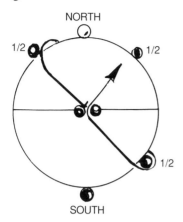

WRAP DIAGONALLY using the 1/2 mark pins to guide. Wrap thread on the side of the pin nearest the North or South Pole. (Figure 8)

Wrap once diagonally around to the LEFT and back to the Keeper Pins.

Fig. 9

Go through the Keepers. Turn the thread inside the Keeper Pins and wrap toward the RIGHT 1/8 Mark Pin. Continue around the ball. End where you began, completing the 2 diagonal wraps. (Figure 9)

Fig. 10

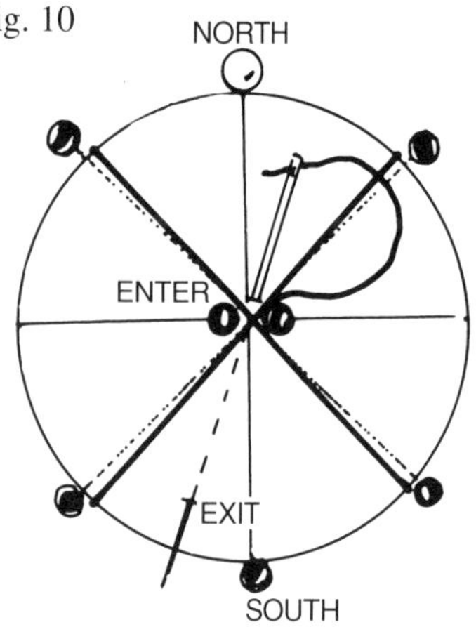

TO END, ENTER the needle between the Keeper Pins. Exit and Escape Downward. (Figure 10)

Fig. 11

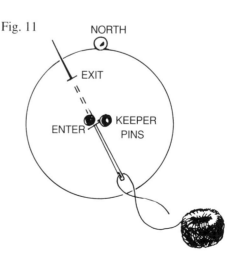

SECOND ROWS: Black DMC #310.

Thread needle with the Black thread. ENTER needle BETWEEN the KEEPER PINS to EXIT UPWARD. (Figure 11)

Fig. 12

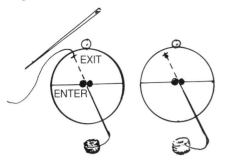

Pull needle and thread through.

Remove needle from thread.
Pull thread end back until it disappears
under ball's surface. (Figure 12)

Thread is now attached to the ball,
coming out between the Keeper Pins.
(Figure 13)

Fig. 13

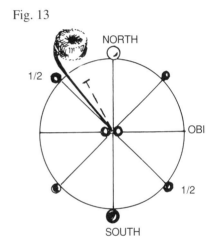

NOTE: When thread is *pre-measured*
and *pre-cut*, ENTER the needle
AWAY (above, below, to the side) so
that it EXITS BETWEEN the Keeper Pins.

When thread is *wrapped onto the ball*
directly from the spool, ENTER
needle BETWEEN the Keeper Pins so that
it EXITS AWAY. (Then remove needle,
pull end under).
Thread will begin the wrap from
between the Keepers.

Wrap DIAGONALLY from the thread spool.

Fig. 14

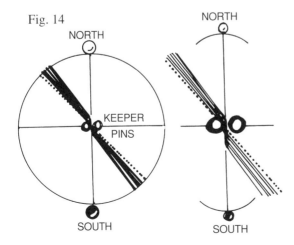

EACH TIME THROUGH THE KEEPER
PINS, the Wrap THREAD CHANGES
FROM ONE SIDE of the MARK LINE
to the OTHER.
THREAD ALWAYS changes to the Pole
SIDE of the PREVIOUS ROW.
Each successive Row becomes nearer
the Pole.(Figure 14)
Keeper Pins create a Center Point from
which all threads RADIATE.

WRAP Black #310:
    5 ROWS to the LEFT,
    5 ROWS to the RIGHT.
  End where you began.(Figure 15)

Fig. 15

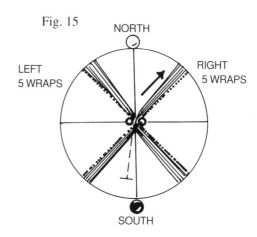

Fig. 16

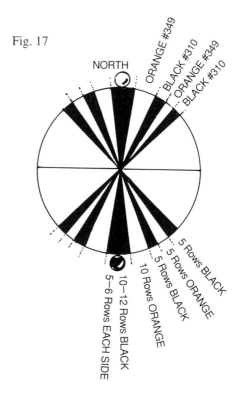

TO END:
  CUT the thread, WITH 6 EXTRA INCHES.
  Thread end into needle.

ENTER needle between the Keeper Pins to
EXIT DOWNWARD.
ESCAPE and cut thread at ball's surface.
(Figure 16)

HOLD the Ball with the NORTH POLE
at the TOP.

THIRD ROWS: Orange #349
    WRAP 5 ROWS LEFT,
    WRAP 5 ROWS RIGHT. (Figure 17)

EXIT and ESCAPE downward.

CONTINUE THE PATTERN:

Wrap BLACK #310:
    5 Rows to the LEFT,
    5 Rows to the RIGHT.

Wrap ORANGE #349:
    10 Rows to the LEFT,
    10 Rows to the Right.

CENTER:
Wrap BLACK #310:
    5 Rows to the LEFT,
    5 Rows to the RIGHT.
FILL CENTER with 2 or 3 extra rows to
cover the Mark Line if necessary.

44

Fig. 18

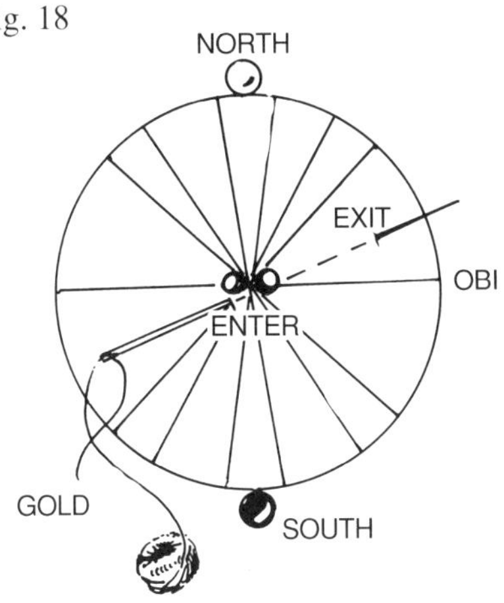

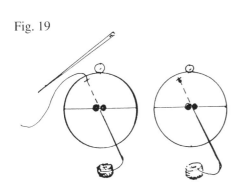

**WRAP GOLD TO OUTLINE
EACH COLOR CHANGE.**
Wrap Gold from the spool.

ENTER needle just BELOW LEFT Keeper Pin to
EXIT away RIGHT of the pattern. (Figure 18)
Pull needle and thread through. Remove needle.
Knot thread's end. Pull knot back through under
ball's surface. (Figure 19)
Start LEFT and work to the RIGHT. (Figure 20)
WRAP 1 Gold Row to outline each group of colored
threads. End where you began.
CUT THREAD from the spool with ABOUT
24 INCHES EXTRA.

Fig. 19

Fig. 20

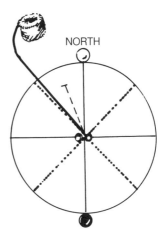

Thread end into needle. ENTER needle under
thread cluster to EXIT on the other side. (Figure 21)
Take a BACK STITCH around the thread cluster
to secure at the Keeper Pins, on the Obi Line.
Continue to Backstitch around the cluster
— 4 stitches ABOVE the Obi, and 4 stitches
BELOW the Obi Line. (Figure 22)

Fig. 21

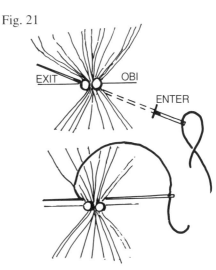

Fig. 22

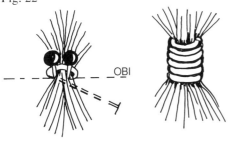

BACKSTITCH the cluster on the OPPOSITE
SIDE of the ball, 5 stitches Above the Obi,
5 stitches Below.

Fig. 23

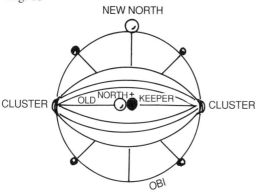

NEW NORTH

CLUSTER — OLD NORTH + KEEPER — CLUSTER

OBI

Fig. 24

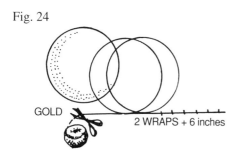

GOLD

2 WRAPS + 6 inches

FIRST ROWS — GOLD Metallic

MEASURE and CUT 2 WRAPS plus 6 inches.
Thread needle, KNOT the end. (Figure 24)

ENTER AWAY to EXIT between Keepers.
(Figure 25)
Across thread wrap pattern #1,
Wrap DIAGONALLY — 1 ROW LEFT,
1 ROW RIGHT. End where you began,
ENTER BETWEEN Keeper Pins to EXIT
DOWNWARD and Escape.

CONTINUE THE PATTERN —
Begin each time by holding the NEW
North Pole at TOP, OLD North Pole
points at your nose.

Wrap thread from the spool.
Enter between Keeper Pins to Exit
Upward each time.

WRAP DIRECTION #2:

Now CHANGE the PINS.
Hold the ball so the North Pole points
at your nose and GREEN Stripes run
HORIZONTAL. (Figure 23)
NORTH POLE now becomes Keeper Pins
— ADD A PIN to the North Pole pin.
SOUTH POLE is the OPPOSITE Keeper
— ADD a PIN to the South Pole pin.
The NEW Keeper Pins run HORIZONTAL in
the CENTER of the HORIZONTAL Black Line.

Remove the pins at marked intersections.
Replace pins at the new marked intersection
on the Obi Line.
Place a New North Pole at the Obi Line at
whichever end is up.
(It's just to mark your beginning and help keep
your place).

Fig. 25

NEW
NORTH

1/8   1/8

EXIT

1/8   ENTER   1/8

GOLD

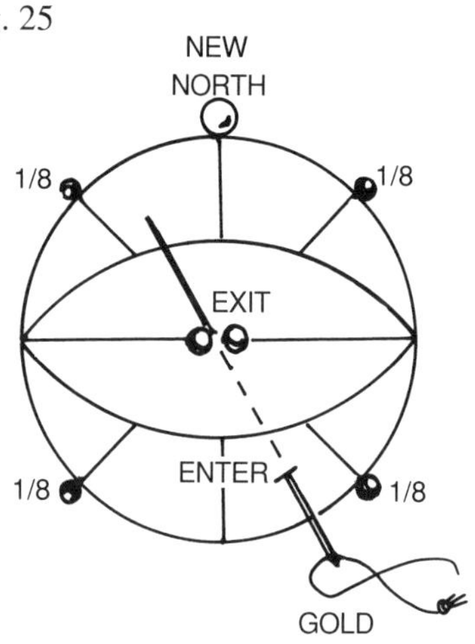

WRAP Black #310:
    5 ROWS — Left, Right.
Magenta #915:
    5 ROWS — Left, Right.
Black #310:
    5 ROWS — Left, Right.
Magenta #915:
    10 ROWS — Left, Right.
Black #310:
    5 ROWS — Left, Right.
Add 2-3 Black rows if necessary to cover.

Fig. 26

WRAP GOLD to divide each color section. Cut Gold thread with 24 inches extra and backstitch both thread clusters. (Figure 26)

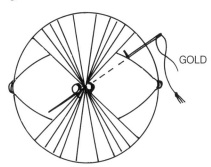

GOLD

WRAP DIRECTION #3

REPLACE Keeper Pins SIDE BY SIDE along the CENTER BLACK LINE of the MAGENTA SECTIONS.(Figure 27)

In Wrap Direction #3, ALL WRAPS are applied with the NEEDLE. The needle brings each wrap OVER, UNDER, OVER, UNDER the Orange Section.
The order of threads remains the same.

Fig. 27

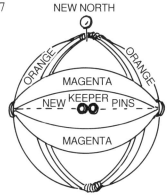

NEW NORTH

ORANGE   ORANGE

MAGENTA

NEW KEEPER PINS

MAGENTA

To begin, MEASURE GOLD Metallic — 2 wraps plus 6 inches. (Figure 28)

Fig. 28

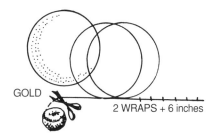

GOLD

2 WRAPS + 6 inches

Fig. 29

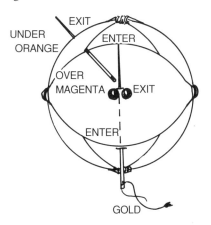

EXIT

UNDER ORANGE

ENTER

OVER MAGENTA   EXIT

ENTER

GOLD

ENTER AWAY to EXIT BETWEEN Keeper Pins. (Figure 29)

Go OVER the MAGENTA Section
DIAGONALLY to the Corner of the
Green Section. (Figure 30)
ENTER needle at the corner of
the Orange Section. GO UNDER the
Orange Section (a long reach under)
to EXIT at its OTHER CORNER.
Go OVER MAGENTA, through Keepers,
to the corner of the opposite green section.
Go under Orange again and Exit. Go back
to Keepers and wrap DIAGONALLY the
other direction — Over Magenta Sections,
Under Orange Sections and back again.

Catch the Gold thread at the Keeper Pins
intersection. Exit and Escape.

INSERT a NEW North Pole, to help mark
your place. Hold the New North Pole at
the TOP.

Fig. 30

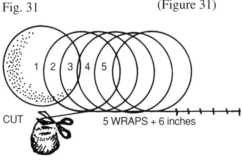

THE PATTERN:

BLACK #310:
   Pre-measure and cut
   — 5 WRAPS plus 6 INCHES each time.
   (Figure 31)

Fig. 31

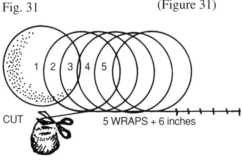

Fig. 32

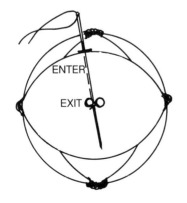

Thread needle. ENTER ABOVE to EXIT
BETWEEN Keepers.(Figure 32)

Fig. 33

Start LEFT. Do 5 Rows OVER Magenta,
UNDER Orange. Exit, Escape. (Figure 33)

Fig. 34

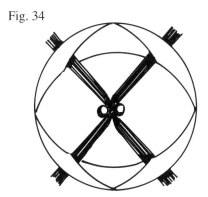

BLACK #310:
    MEASURE 5 more Wraps plus 6 inches.
    Do 5 ROWS to the RIGHT,
    OVER Magenta, UNDER Orange.
    (Figure 34)

GREEN #991:
    MEASURE 5 wraps plus 6 inches.
    Do 5 ROWS LEFT.
    MEASURE and Cut.
    Do 5 ROWS RIGHT.

BLACK #310:
    Measure and Cut.
    Do 5 ROWS LEFT,
    5 ROWS RIGHT.

GREEN #991:
    10 ROWS — LEFT, RIGHT.
    Do 5 rows at a time.
Do NOT try to use 10 wraps of thread.
Use 5 WRAPS plus 6 inches and REPEAT
TWICE alternating sides.

BLACK #310:
    6 ROWS — LEFT, RIGHT.
    Measure 6 WRAPS plus 6 inches twice.
    Complete the center stripe.

GOLD — Measure 4 WRAPS plus 6 inches
    — DO HALF from Outside to Center.
Measure 4 WRAPS plus 24 inches.
Complete the outlines, Center to Other Side.
Stitch the 2 Clusters.

The ball is complete.

Big Diamonds Obi

This is the traditional version. Actually a wide Obi pattern, this ball uses big overlapping diamonds to create its design. An uncomplicated pattern, it is created with color units repeated in numerical order. Long stitches make it easy to complete in a short time.

MATERIALS:

4 inch Styrofoam ball — Navy Blue thread wrap

DMC Pearl Cotton #5 in 3 colors:
   Turquoise #943
   Light Gray #762
   Red Orange #606

Kreinik's 1/16 inch Metallic Ribbon in 2 colors:
   Copper #027 — 3 Spools
   Turquoise #029 — 1 Spool

Kreinik's Very Fine Braid #4 — Copper #021 — 1 Spool

INSTRUCTIONS:

DIVIDE the ball into 8ths with an Obi. (Figure 1)

MARK the divisions with Kreinik's Very Fine Braid Copper #021.

TACK the North and South Poles.
TACK the Obi Line intersections. (Figure 2)

Fig. 1

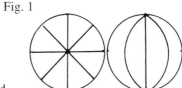

8 Divisions

Fig. 3

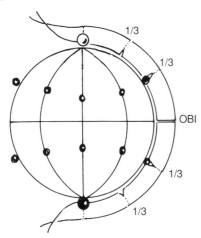

Fig. 2

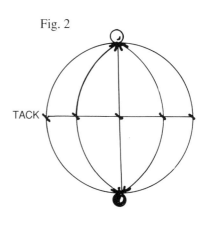

From OBI to POLES, DIVIDE ALL 8 Mark Lines 1/3 ABOVE the Obi Line and 1/3 BELOW the Obi Line. MARK the 1/3s with PINS. (Figure 3)

Fig. 4

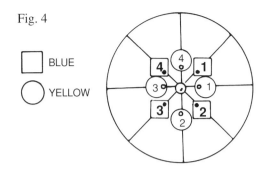

☐ BLUE

◯ YELLOW

Make 2 SETS of paper tabs numbered 1, 2, 3, 4.
Use 2 colors of pins, YELLOW and BLUE.
(Figure 4)

Hold the ball with the North Pole TOP.
The paper tabs are placed around the
NORTH POLE. Use one set of numbers for
YELLOW PINS, use the other set of tabs
for BLUE PINS.

Starting with the YELLOW Pin and #1,
then BLUE Pin and #1, turn the ball
CLOCKWISE.
Place the paper tabs Yellow 1 — Blue 1,
Yellow 2 — Blue 2, Yellow 3 — Blue 3,
Yellow 4 — Blue 4, ALTERNATING
THE COLORS.

Fig. 5

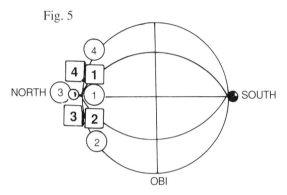

NORTH   SOUTH

OBI

When you start each Diamond Unit,
HOLD THE BALL with the
NORTH POLE on the *LEFT*,
SOUTH POLE on the *RIGHT*.
(Figure 5)

Each DIAMOND UNIT is either
1 ROW Kreinik's COPPER 1/16 inch Ribbon #027
and
3 ROWS DMC Pearl Cotton Light Gray #762.

TOP — START POINTS of Gray Diamonds
begin on Mark Lines with YELLOW PINS.

OR

1 ROW Kreinik's COPPER 1/16 inch Ribbon #027
and
3 ROWS DMC Pearl Cotton Turquoise #943.

TOP — START POINTS of Turquoise Diamonds
begin on Mark Lines with BLUE PINS.
(Figure 6)

Fig. 6

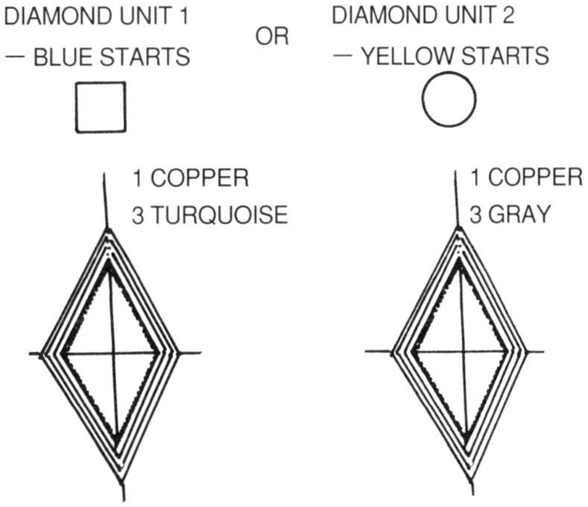

DIAMOND UNIT 1   OR   DIAMOND UNIT 2
— BLUE STARTS   — YELLOW STARTS

☐   ◯

1 COPPER   1 COPPER
3 TURQUOISE   3 GRAY

DIAMOND POINTS OVERLAP AT THE
OBI LINE INTERSECTIONS.

COMPLETE ONE TOTAL UNIT EACH TIME
BEFORE GOING ON TO THE NEXT.

DO NOT do just the COPPER ON ALL
4 DIAMONDS and then the color or the design
will not be correct.

START each diamond AT THE OBI LINE,
hold the ball — NORTH LEFT,
SOUTH RIGHT, OBI TOP.

51

Fig. 7

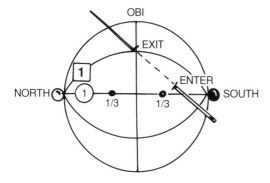

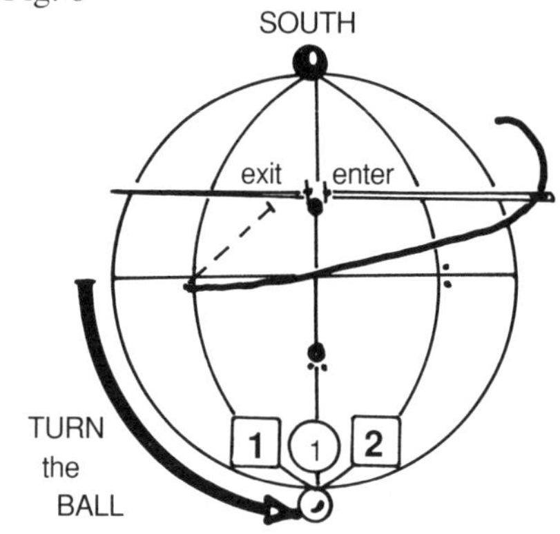

As you stitch the Diamonds, turn the ball around the pattern with each stitch COUNTER-CLOCKWISE (around to the left). (Figures 7 through 12)

Fig. 8

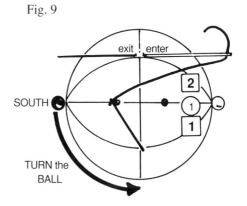

Fig. 9

Fig. 10

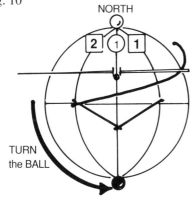

Fig. 11

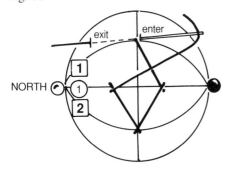

Fig. 12

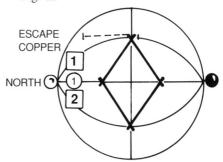

TURQUOISE DIAMONDS USE THE
BLUE PINS.
START with the NUMBER 1.
COMPLETE the Diamond Unit,
    1 Row Copper 1/16 inch Ribbon,
    3 Rows of DMC Turquoise #943.

Keep POINT STITCHES CLOSE
TOGETHER on the Obi Line.

Fig. 13

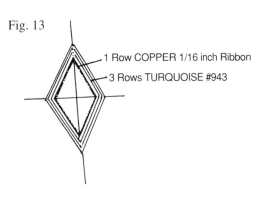

1 Row COPPER 1/16 inch Ribbon
3 Rows TURQUOISE #943

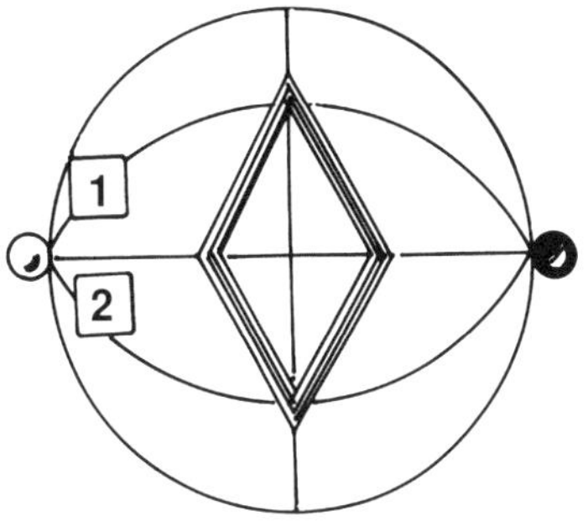

Go to BLUE PIN NUMBER 2,
complete the TURQUOISE Unit.
(Figures 15, 16)

Fig. 14

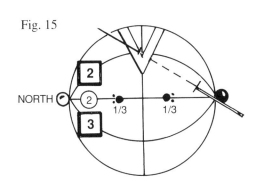

Fig. 15

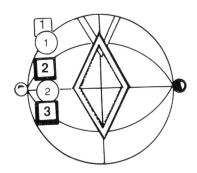

NORTH

Fig. 16

Then go to PIN 3, then to PIN 4.

TURN the ball AWAY from you each time
a unit is completed.(Figure 17)

Fig. 17

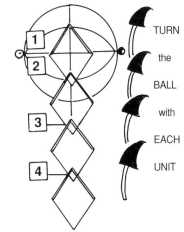

TURN
the
BALL
with
EACH
UNIT

Fig. 18

When all 4 TURQUOISE Diamond Units are
completed, BEGIN at YELLOW PIN
NUMBER 1 with GRAY DIAMOND
UNITS.(Figure 18)
Go on to 2, 3, 4 at YELLOW PINS.

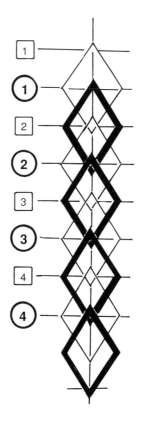

Around the OBI LINE, MARK the CENTERS
HALF WAY between each of the Division Lines
with a pin. This will help to space the Points
of the Diamonds as they grow into the Centers of
each division along the Obi Line. (Figure 19)

Fig. 19

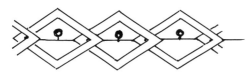

1 LAYER = 4 Turquoise Diamond Units
plus 4 Light Gray Diamond Units.

Do 4 LAYERS (4 Diamond units, one outside
the last).
Diamond POINTS OVERLAP EACH OTHER
over the Division lines at the Obi.
They become larger and larger with each
Layer.

LAYER #4 — Space so FINAL POINTS ARE
EQUAL in the CENTERS of all sections.
There will be space left over in the Centers
around the Obi Line.

LAYER #5-A: TURQUOISE Final Unit
    1 ROW COPPER 1/16 inch Ribbon #027
    2 ROWS DMC Red Orange #606
around all 4 Turquoise Diamonds.

The Obi pattern is complete.

LAYER #5-B: LIGHT GRAY Final Unit
    1 ROW COPPER 1/16 inch Ribbon #027
    2 ROWS DMC Turquoise #943
    1 ROW METALLIC TURQUOISE
        1/16 inch Ribbon #029.

STARBURST:

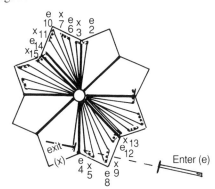

Fig. 20

In the space around the North and South Poles, stitch a Starburst using the "PINE NEEDLE STITCH."

Use Kreinik's COPPER metallic Very Fine Braid #4, color #021.

Start at the NORTH POLE END.
Thread needle with a long length of thread.
Knot the end.

ENTER to EXIT just LEFT of a Mark Line,
JUST INSIDE the Diamonds pattern. (Figure 20)

Fig. 21

Use the NORTH POLE PIN to PIVOT THREAD around as the Center intersection is crossed each time. (Figure 21)

Fig. 22

TACK The CENTERS

Take all OUTER STITCHES JUST INSIDE the PATTERN THREADS,
about 1/4 inch (1/2 cm) apart.

Follow the numbers in the diagram.

SKIP OVER MARK THREAD and go on to the next section.

Continue back and forth across the center.

Fill in all sections.

Repeat the Starburst at the SOUTH POLE end.

The ball is complete.

Big Diamonds Simplified

This simplified pattern uses a smaller ball (the original is 4 inches) and flat braided ribbon to speed the completion. Alternating layers of diamonds create the pattern.

MATERIALS:

3 inch ball — Lavender thread wrap

Rhode Island Textiles RibbonFloss™ in 3 colors:
    Deep Purple — "Black Orchid" #142F-26
    Yellow Ochre — "Honey" #142F-17
    White — #142F-2

Rainbow Gallery's "Neon Rays" may be substituted for RibbonFloss™
Rhode Island Textiles Metallic RibbonFloss™
    Silver — #144F-2

Silver metallic Mark thread:
Rhode Island Textiles — Reflection Collection™ metallic braid — Silver #154-2

or Kreinik Balger Ombre — Silver #1000
or Y L I "Candlelight" Silver — no color number

8 Paper Tabs

8 Colored Pins — 4 Blue, 4 Yellow

METHOD:

DIVIDE the ball into 8ths with an Obi. (Figure 1)

MARK the 8ths with Silver Mark Thread.

TACK the North and South Poles. (Figure 2)
TACK the 8 Obi Line Intersections.

FROM OBI TO POLES, DIVIDE ALL 8 Mark Lines 1/3 ABOVE and 1/3 BELOW the Obi Line. Mark the 3rds with pins. (Figure 3)

Fig. 1

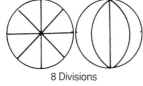

8 Divisions

Fig. 2

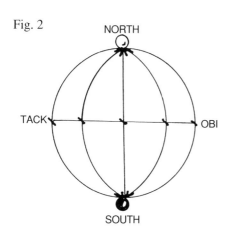

Fig. 3

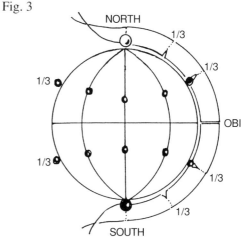

Make 8 Paper Tabs — 2 sets of 4 tabs numbered 1 - 2 - 3 - 4.

Hold the ball North Pole at TOP.

Set the Map.(Figure 4)

Use the Paper Tabs around the North Pole Pin.
Use 2 colors of pins (Blue and Yellow) alternating.

Fig. 4

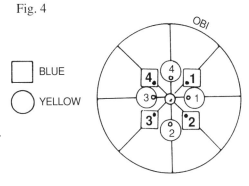

□ BLUE

○ YELLOW

Fig. 5

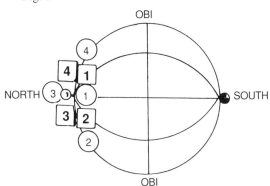

Pin tabs around the North Pole Pin on each Mark Line CLOCKWISE,
        #1 BLUE - #1 YELLOW,
        #2 BLUE - #2 YELLOW,
        #3 BLUE - #3 YELLOW,
        #4 BLUE - #4 YELLOW.

Hold the ball so that the NORTH POLE is on the LEFT, SOUTH POLE is on the RIGHT. **The ball is held in this position TO BEGIN each Diamond.** (Figure 5) Number 1 Tab-BLUE PIN is facing your nose.

THE DIAMOND PATTERN:

1 LAYER IS 4 DIAMONDS.

2 Layers alternate to create the pattern, starting at Blue Pins 1, 2, 3, 4, and starting at Yellow Pins 1, 2, 3, 4.

The TOP POINT of the Diamond starts at the Number Tab line.
The SIDE Points of the Diamond are the 1/3 mark pins.
The BOTTOM of the Diamond is just beyond the next 8th Mark Line.
Each Diamond is stitched outside the last.
Points of the Diamonds overlap at the Obi Line to create the pattern.

Fig. 6

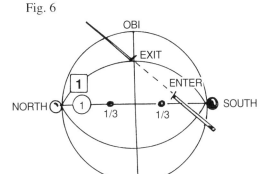

To Stitch the Diamond, start at the TOP of the pattern each time. TURN the ball as you stitch the diamond. Stitching goes Clockwise around the Diamond.

To begin, thread your needle with Silver Metallic RibbonFloss™ #144F-2.
KNOT the END.

ENTER to EXIT JUST LEFT of the OBI LINE, JUST ABOVE the Mark Line numbered 1-Blue Pin.(Figure 6)

Fig. 7

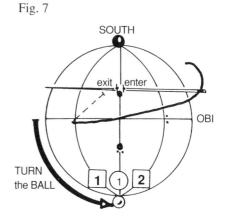

NOTE: AS YOU STITCH the First Rows, REMOVE 1/3 MARK PINS as you take each stitch.
KEEP STITCHES at the OBI LINE CLOSE TOGETHER.
At side corners, allow more generous spacing to prevent ribbon rows from falling on top of each other.
KEEP RIBBON LAID FLAT. MITER CORNERS.

Turn the Ball so the SOUTH POLE is at the TOP.
Take a stitch ABOVE the 1/3 Mark pin.
Remove the 1/3 Mark Pin.(Figure 7)

Fig. 8

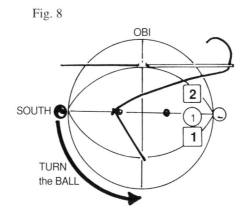

Turn the Ball so the South Pole is on the LEFT.
Take a stitch at the OBI LINE just ABOVE
the 8th mark line. (Figure 8)

Fig. 9

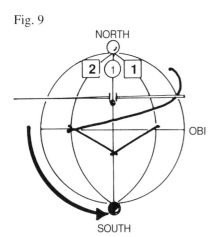

Turn the ball so the South Pole is at the BOTTOM.
Take a stitch ABOVE the opposite 1/3 Mark Pin.
Remove the 1/3 Mark Pin. (Figure 9)

58

Fig. 10

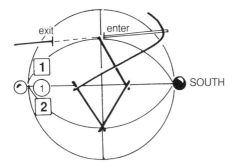

Fig. 11

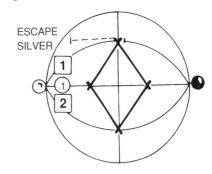

Turn the ball so the South Pole is on the RIGHT.
ENTER to the RIGHT of the Mark Line to
complete the stitch. EXIT and ESCAPE.
Cut the thread. (Figures 10, 11)

Fig. 12

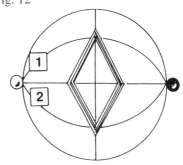

Fig. 13

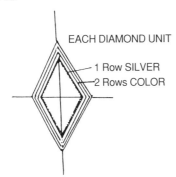

Thread needle with PURPLE RibbonFloss™.
Knot the end.

ENTER to EXIT just ABOVE the last Row and
to the LEFT of the Obi Line.
Turn the ball, South Pole TOP,
continue to stitch 2 Rows of Purple around
the outside of the Silver Diamond. (Figure 12)

Each Diamond has
1 Row Metallic Silver RibbonFloss™ #144F-2
and 2 Rows of RibbonFloss™ color,
total 3 Rows each Diamond. (Figure 13)

Fig. 14

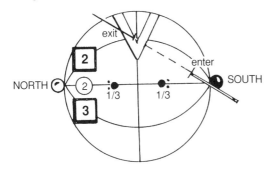

Now go to Blue Pin #2, (Figures 14, 15)

Fig. 15

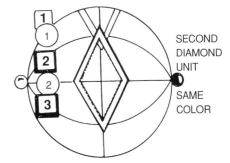

Fig. 16

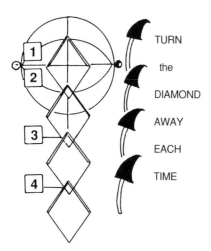

TURN

the

DIAMOND

AWAY

EACH

TIME

then Blue Pin #3, then Blue Pin #4. (Figure 16)

Then Begin at Yellow Pin #1, Yellow #2, Yellow #3, Yellow #4.(Figure 17)

Follow the pattern.

THE PATTERN from the Beginning:

BLUE PINS 1 — 4
1 Row Silver Metallic
    RibbonFloss™ #144F-2
2 Rows Purple "Black Orchid"
    RibbonFloss™ #142F-26

YELLOW PINS 1 — 4
1 Row Silver Metallic
    RibbonFloss™ #144F-2
2 Rows "Honey" RibbonFloss #142F-17

BLUE PINS 1 — 4
1 Row Silver RibbonFloss™ #144F-2
2 Rows Purple "Black Orchid"
    RibbonFloss™ #142F-26

YELLOW PINS 1 — 4
1 Row Silver Metallic
    RibbonFloss #144F-2
2 Rows "Honey" RibbonFloss #142F-17

BLUE PINS 1 — 4
1 Row Silver RibbonFloss #144F-2
2 Rows Purple "Black Orchid"
    RibbonFloss #142F-26

YELLOW PINS 1 — 4
1 Row Silver RibbonFloss #144F-2
2 Rows WHITE RibbonFloss #142F-2

BLUE PINS 1 — 4
1 Row WHITE RibbonFloss #142F-2.

Fig. 17

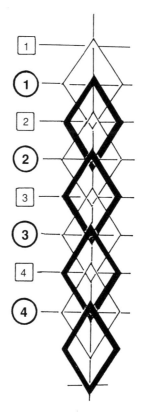

Fig. 18

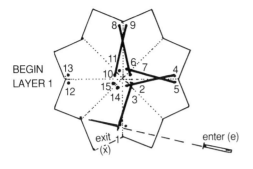

BEGIN
LAYER 1

NORTH AND SOUTH POLE STARS:

To complete this ball, use the 8 Mark Lines
around the North and South Poles to stitch an
8 pointed Star using the KIKU Stitch.
Use the Silver Metallic RibbonFloss #144F-2.
Do 1 Row only.

ENTER to EXIT at the Point of a Diamond. (Figure 18)
Do Inside stitches CLOSE to the Pole intersection.
Do OUTSIDE POINT stitches at POINTS
of the Diamond pattern. (Figures 19, 20)

Fig. 19

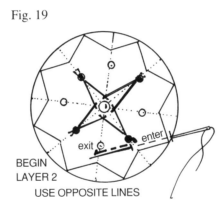

BEGIN
LAYER 2
USE OPPOSITE LINES

Fig. 20

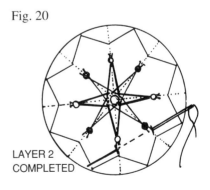

LAYER 2
COMPLETED

The ball is complete.

Ball #5

Window Ball
With Appliqué

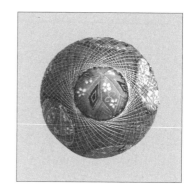

This variation uses patterned fabric cut-outs stitched to the ball's surface. The Window pattern is wrapped on top.

Fabrics with patterns that are isolated (not overlapping) work best. Small flowers, fish or birds, or geometric patterns work as items in a basket or cage. Mine are Temari — fabric-covered balls from Japanese printed cotton.

Embroidery of small motifs is equally effective.

MATERIALS:

3 inch ball wrapped in a double thread combination wrap of saddle brown and Sulky metallic embroidery thread — variegated in copper, pink, and green

Cotton fabric with small patterns — around 1 inch diameter

DMC Metallic Gold — fil or clair

YLI "Candlelight" Metallic — Midnight — dark with variegated colors

Dressmaker Pins

Sharp Long Needle — Milliner's

Fig. 1

TACK

4 DIVISIONS

METHOD:

DIVIDE the ball into 4ths with an Obi Line. (Figure 1)

MARK with 3 wraps of sewing thread, same color as the thread wrap (Invisible Mark).

TACK the North, South and Obi Line intersections.

Fig. 2

CUT out the Appliqué shapes with 1/2 inch Margin around the outside of each. (Figure 2)

With your scissors, CLIP the edges about every 1/2 inch around the outside margin up to the pattern's boundary.

Fig. 3

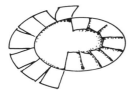

TURN the EDGES UNDER and
shape the piece by folding the margin
under and rounding the curves.
Pin to the ball with dressmaker pins.
(Figures 3, 4)

Fig. 4

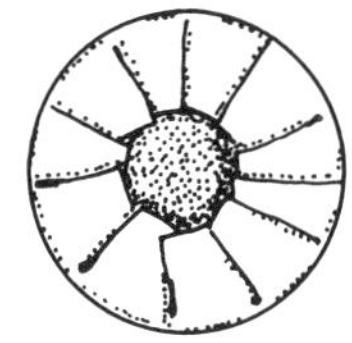

Fig. 5

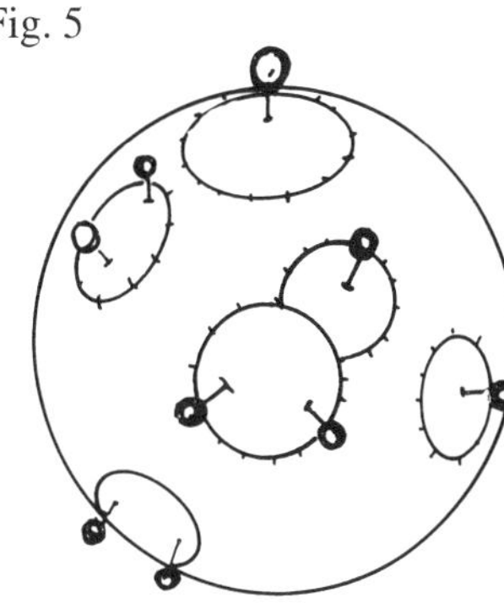

Compose the design and pin the shapes onto
the ball.
If you place shapes at the North and South
Poles, cut your Paper Template to fit over
them. (Figure 5)

When all of the shapes are placed on the ball,
Blind stitch to the ball's surface.
Use sewing thread to match the thread wrap or
the fabric, whichever is the closer match.

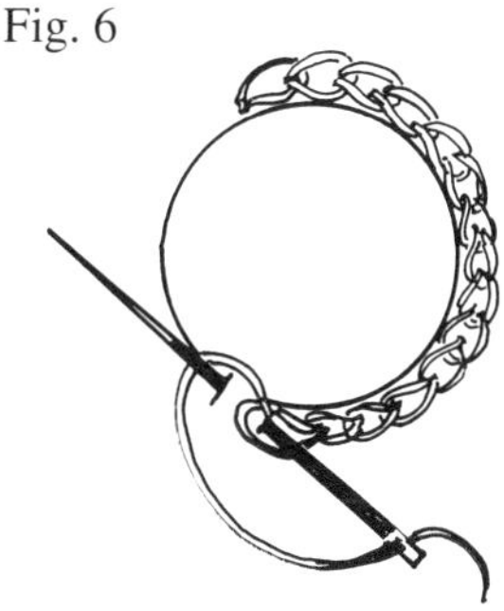

WHEN ALL SHAPES ARE STITCHED
TO THE BALL,
Chain stitch an outline around each of the
appliquéd shapes.
Use the "Candlelight" Metallic — Midnight
(Black with variegated colors). (Figure 6)

Fig. 6

Fig. 7

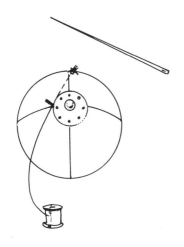

MATERIAL for Window Wrap on Appliqué ball:
Use 1 STRAND of DMC GOLD fil or clair.
Pull the thread taut over the ball's surface.

GO TO PAGE 65. Use FIGURES 9 through 15
to Wrap on the Window pattern over the Appliqué.
END on PAGE 66.
WRAP LAYER 2 is NOT USED on the Appliqué
Ball.

Pin the North and South Pole circle templates to the
ball as your wrapping guides. (Figure 7)

Instructions follow on page 65.

Basic "Window" Wrapped Ball

This design is ripe for experimentation. Wrapped rows of thread are spaced evenly apart around the Obi Line. The North and South Pole ends use a circle template to shape the open space.

This pattern is fast and easy. It can used over a fabric covered surface or over a thread wrap of sewing thread wrapped together with metallic machine embroidery thread for extra fire.

The second variation consists of two wrapped layers, the evenly spaced threads of Layer 1 and a second layer of 4 wrapped Obi bands of contrasting color.

The color of the ball is the "Window" so it should coordinate with the selected color combination of the wrap threads.

Try a thread wrap in a medium shade, then use either lighter or darker contrasting design threads. This design works equally wellon 2 1/2, 3 or 4 inch balls.

MATERIALS:

3 inch ball with Light Chartreuse thread wrap
Save some thread for the "Invisible Mark"

Aqua Blue Metallic "Candlelight"

"Jewel" Hologram filament Gold #525 by Madeira
(Article #9843)

WRAP LAYER #1:
Aqua Blue Metallic "Candlelight" thread and
"Jewel" Hologram Gold #525 thread are wrapped together.

WRAP LAYER #2:
DMC Bright Silver "Fil argent ml fin" #10
    OR TRY a Contrasting but coordinating non-metallic thread like DMC Flower Thread or DMC Pearl Cotton #12 may be substituted for the Silver Metallic DMC.

Plain White Paper and scissors

This design uses 2 circle templates at the North and South Poles.
Sizes:
    for 3 inch ball — circle diameter 4 cm
    for 2 1/2 inch ball — circle diameter 3 1/2 cm
    for 4 inch ball — circle diameter 7 cm

METHOD:

DIVIDE the ball into 4ths around the Obi.
(Figure 8)

"INVISIBLE MARK": MARK the 4ths and Obi Line
with 3 wraps of the sewing thread wrap.

TACK the North and South Poles and the Obi
at the 1/4 intersections.

Fig. 8

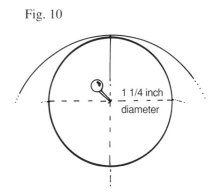

Fig. 9

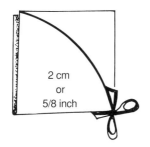

2 cm
or
5/8 inch

CUT 2 PAPER CIRCLES - fold paper into 1/4s.
Measure the radius from the center in several
places.
Cut the circle. (Figure 9)

Place another NORTH POLE PIN through the CENTER
of the CIRCLE. Use the folded INTERSECTION
to place the pin.
Place another SOUTH POLE PIN through the
CENTER of the other circle. (Figure 10)

PIN THE CIRCLES TO THE BALL AT THE EXACT
NORTH and SOUTH Poles, replacing the original
North and South Pole Pins.

Fig. 10

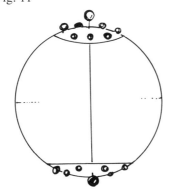

1 1/4 inch
diameter

Fig. 11

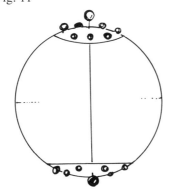

Use about 8 pins to pin down the circles edges
flat against the ball. (Figure 11)

WRAP LAYER #1: Aqua Blue "Candlelight" and "Jewel" Hologram Gold #525.

Thread your needle from the 2 spools, one strand of each. (Figure 12)

ENTER your NEEDLE just outside the circle template at the North Pole at a 1/4 Mark Line to EXIT away. Remove the needle, KNOT the threads' ends. Pull the threads back until the knot disappears. (Figure 13)

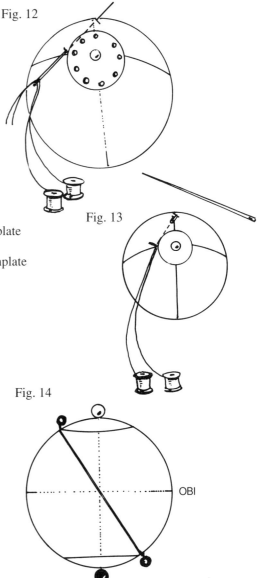

Fig. 12

Fig. 13

Wrap onto the ball from the 2 spools.
Each wrap of the design will use the template North and South as guidelines.
Each Row will border the edge of the template to create the "Window." (Figure 14)

Continue the wrap around the ball to the OPPOSITE DIVISION LINE at the South Pole end and back to the North to complete.
Back at the North Pole, the wrap goes slightly beyond the start point.
Continue wrap number 2 in the same direction to lay approximately 1 cm to the RIGHT on the Obi Line. (Figure 15)

Fig. 14

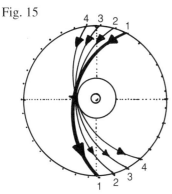

Fig. 15

Fig. 16

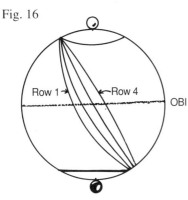

Wrap evenly spaced lines 1 cm apart at the Obi Line continuing until the ball is covered.
Wrap around the outside of the template at top and bottom. (Figure 16)
Overlapping wraps will create a diamond pattern.
Keep wraps spaced by checking diamond shapes and sizes.

When the Layer One wraps are completed, cut the thread from the spools with 6 inches extra. Thread ends into needle. Hide the finish at the top edge of the circle template. ENTER, EXIT, and ESCAPE.

The APPLIQÚE BALL is complete at this point.

Fig. 17

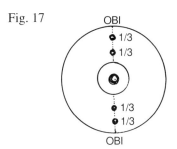

WRAP LAYER #2 — a wrapped Obi:
Shiny Silver DMC fil argent ml fin #10 and "Candlelight" Aqua Blue metallic.

Replace Obi Line Mark pins at 2 OPPOSITE 1/4 Mark Lines. (Figure 17)

DIVIDE 2 OPPOSITE Mark Lines into 3rds between the edge of the circle template and the Obi Line, North and South. (Figure 18)

Begin Diagonal wrap #1 at the Obi line. Use the Division pins nearest the Obi Line for the first band. (Figure 19)
Thread your needle with DMC Silver fil argent ml fin #10. ENTER at the Obi Line to EXIT away.
Remove the needle. Knot the end.
Pull the knot back through.

Fig. 18

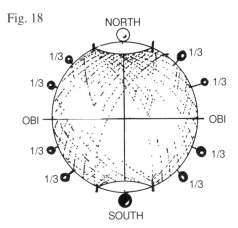

WRAP FLAT WITHOUT CROSSOVERS and KEEPER PINS until threads form a band about 1/8 inch wide, about 10 Rows. End at the Obi Line. Enter, Exit and Escape.

Second Wrap — use the pins at the same level on the opposite side and wrap to the other side.

Third and Fourth Wraps — use the pins nearest the Circle Templates. Wrap diagonally to the Left, and to the Right.

Now turn the ball 1/4 turn.(Figure 20)
Mark the 1/3s Above and Below the Obi on the remaining division line.
Repeat the wraps.

Fig. 19

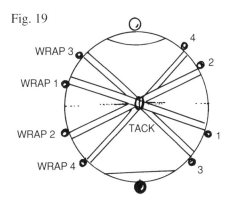

Fig. 20

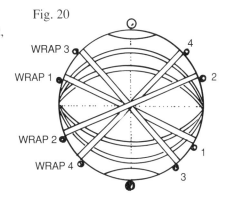

Fig. 21

With 2 or 3 stitches, TACK the center intersections of the outer wraps. (Figure 21)

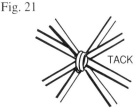

67

Fig. 22

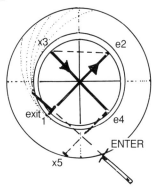

NORTH AND SOUTH POLE STARS

Finish with 8 pointed stars using KIKU STITCH.

Use Metallic Aqua Blue to ADD 2 MORE DIVISION LINES at the Pole Intersections to make 8 DIVISIONS. (Figure 22)

Fig. 23

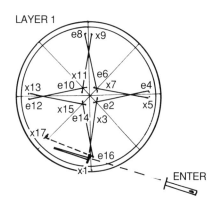

Use Metallic Aqua Blue "Candlelight" to stitch 3 Rows of Kiku Stitch alternating on 4 points each row. (Figures 23, 24)

Fig. 24

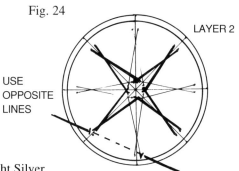

Outline the star with 2 ROWS of DMC Bright Silver "fil argent ml fin" #10. Do alternating rows on the 2 sets of 4 points to complete 2 rows on all. (Figure 25)

The ball is complete.

Fig. 25

ON EACH LINE:
3 Rows AQUA "Candlelight"

2 Rows SILVER DMC #10

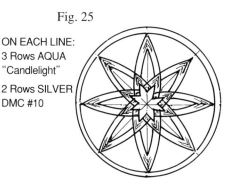

The Double Eighths Mark

The DOUBLE EIGHTHS
MARK SYMBOL

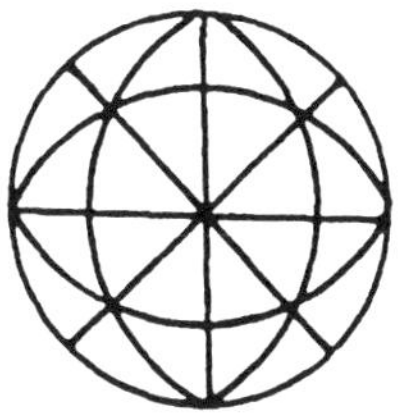

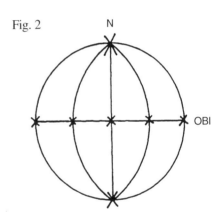

Fig. 1

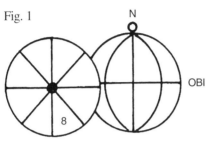

Divide into 8ths with an OBI LINE.

Fig. 2

TACK all 8 intersections around the Obi, and the NORTH and SOUTH POLES.

Fig. 3

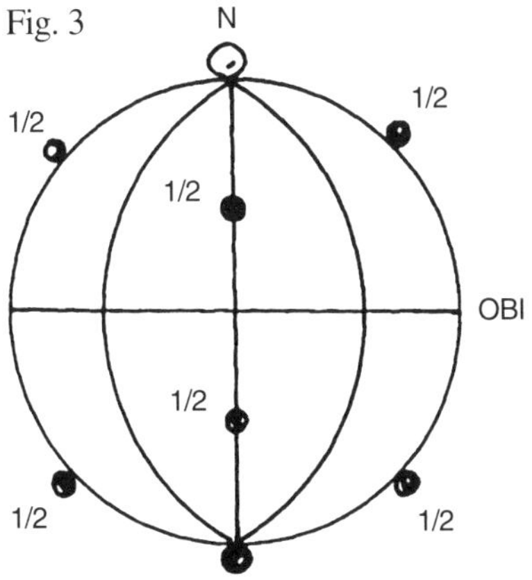

Divide every other line in 1/2 between NORTH and OBI and SOUTH and OBI.
Mark with pins.

Fig. 4

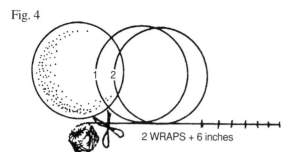

2 WRAPS + 6 inches

MEASURE 2 WRAPS plus 6 inches of marking thread.

Fig. 6

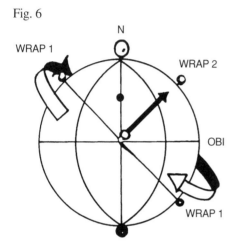

WRAP the thread diagonally (at a 45 degree angle) to the 1/2 mark pin on the LEFT, then continue around the ball.
TURN the direction of the thread at the Start Pin and wrap to the RIGHT.

Fig. 8

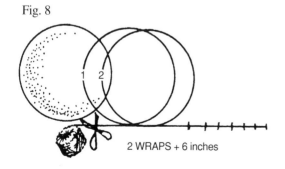

2 WRAPS + 6 inches

MEASURE 2 more WRAPS plus 6 inches of marking thread.

Fig. 5

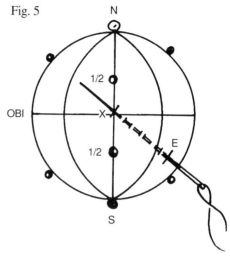

ENTER the needle so that it EXITS at the OBI LINE and an intersection of one 1/2 MARKED LINE.

Fig. 7

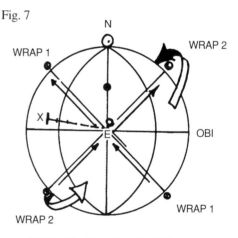

END at the Start Pin. TACK.
EXIT and ESCAPE the needle.

Fig. 9

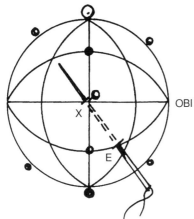

TURN the ball a QUARTER TURN.
ENTER to EXIT at the OBI and
a 1/2 marked intersection.

Fig. 10

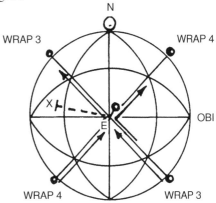

WRAP DIAGONALLY to LEFT
and RIGHT.
END and EXIT.

TACK DIAGONAL INTERSECTIONS
at OBI.

Fig. 11

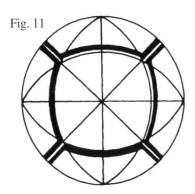

Fig. 12

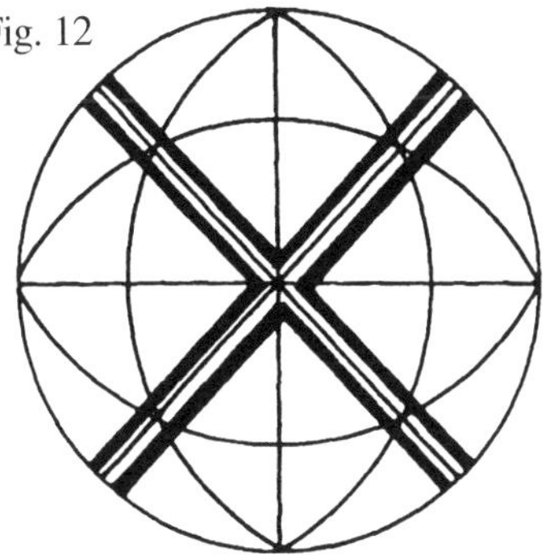

This mark is symmetrical.
It provides 6 EQUAL SQUARES
and 8 EQUAL TRIANGLES,
4 NORTH and 4 SOUTH.

Fig. 13

This is the Double Eighths Mark symbol.

Ribbon Ball   "**Christmas Fire**"

Another simple Ribbon Ball design uses metallic thread to shine the ball's surface. This time only 4 strips of ribbon create the pattern.

MATERIALS:

3 inch ball — Red thread wrap

Red Sulky "Sliver Metallic" #145-8014

5/8 inch Ribbon — this is Gold Paisley on Black background.
4 strips measure 1 wrap + 1 and 1/2 inches
For a 3 inch ball = 1 and 1/2 yards

Mill Hill's "Crystal Treasures" 12 Margarita Crystal AB #13001

Straight Pins

Mark thread — extra Red Sewing Thread

Paper strip

METHOD:

WRAP the ball with Red Sewing Thread to cover yarn. Then combine with Sulky "Sliver Metallic" #145-8014.
Wrap the 2 spools together.

To finish thread cover, stitch several large Zig Zags over the ball's surface to hold the metallic in place.

DIVIDE the ball into 8ths.

MARK with RED SEWING THREAD. Do an Invisible Wrap with 2 wraps at each division.

TACK the North, South and Obi Line Intersections.

DIVIDE the ball into DOUBLE EIGHTHS.
MARK with Red Sewing thread.
Tack the Diagonal Intersections.
(Figures 1 through 3)

Fig. 1

8 Divisions

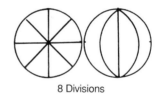
Fig. 2

Fig. 3

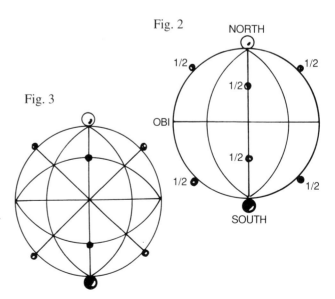

CUT the RIBBON:

4 STRIPS of Ribbon measure 1 Wrap around
the ball plus 1 and 1/2 inches.
After strips are cut, lay them side by side.
Make sure the pattern in the Ribbon is all
going the same direction.

Hold the ball so the North Pole points
at your nose.
Use the Mark Lines around the North Pole
that make a SQUARE. (Figure 4)

Fig. 4

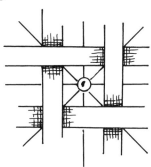

Fig. 5

Place the 4 strips on the Square around the
North Pole at about their middles.
Ends will hang down.(Figure 5)

Use the Mark Lines to align and Center the
widths of the ribbons.

PIN tentatively with 2 pins along the Mark Line.
(Figure 6)

Overlap their corners, LEFT OVER RIGHT.

Fig. 6

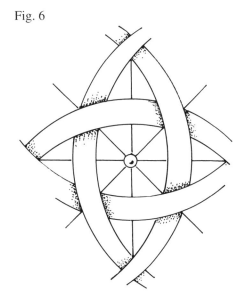

73

At the Obi Line around the ball, WEAVE
the Ribbons. Place a tentative pin on the
Triangular Weave at the Obi Line Intersection.
(Figures 7, 8)

Fig. 7

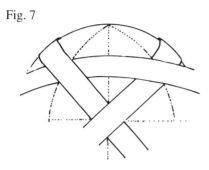

Fig. 8

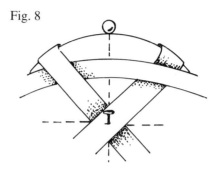

On the South Pole side, Ribbon ends will be
pulled back to the next closest.
Ends are hidden underneath.

Fig. 9

Unpin 1 Ribbon at a time and slide it backwards
just enough so the overlap end slides
1/4 to 1/2 inch under. (Figure 9)

Pin the end before pulling back.
As you pull back, check the Mark lines.
Use them to guide.

Fig. 10

Back the slack around the ball.
Pull the Ribbon Taut and Pin with 2 Pins.

Hide the pins. Slide the Top Ribbon Aside
to pin underneath.

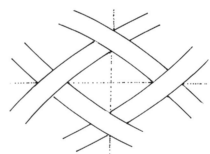

Use Mark Lines as Guides to keep ribbon
placement. Do each of the 4 Ribbons.
(Figure 10)

Pull aside a ribbon, insert pins then replace
the ribbon on top.

The pattern of Ribbons at the South Pole end
is the same.
Ribbon Corners go RIGHT OVER LEFT.

Reinforcement pins may be placed at any
intersections in the same way:
    Pull aside the ribbon,
    Insert 2 pins. Push them flat into the ball.
    Replace the ribbon on top.

The ball is embellished with Mill Hill's
"Crystal Treasures" 12 Margarita Crystal AB
#13001.
The Jewels are PINNED to the ball with
Straight Pins in the Centers of the 4 Diamond
shapes around the Obi and in the Centers of
the 8 Triangles created by the Ribbon pattern
North and South.

A hanging loop is stitched from the North
Pole end.

The ball is complete.

Ribbon Ball   "Royal Renaissance"

"ROYAL RENAISSANCE" uses the stitched lattice pattern of the "Antiquity" ball, the traditional version of this design in the next chapter.

MATERIALS:

3 inch ball Deep Blue Violet thread wrap to match Sulky "Sliver Metallic" #145-8016

3 1/2 yards Gold patterned ribbon 3/8 inch wide to coordinate with Purple thread wrap

Rhode Island Textiles Metallic RibbonFloss™ Light Purple

Mill Hill's "Crystal Treasures" — 12 Margaritas — Topaz AB #13007

Needle — Yarn Darner #18

Paper strip

Straight pins (Dressmaker)

Fig. 1

DOUBLE 8 THS
DIVISION

METHOD:

A 3-inch ball is wrapped with sewing thread then combined with metallic machine embroidery thread. Large Zig Zag stitches over the surface hold it in place while handling.

DIVIDE the ball into 8ths with an Obi Line. Use your paper measure.

MARK the 8ths North to South and the Obi Line with contrasting colored sewing thread — this is a guideline.
The Mark thread will be covered by the Ribbon.

TACK the North, South and Obi Line Intersections.

MARK the Double Eighths with contrasting sewing thread. (Figure 1)

TACK the Obi Line DIAGONAL INTERSECTIONS.

MEASURE and CUT the Ribbon:
    Measure 1 Wrap around the ball plus 1 inch.
    CUT 9 STRIPS of Ribbon to this measurement.

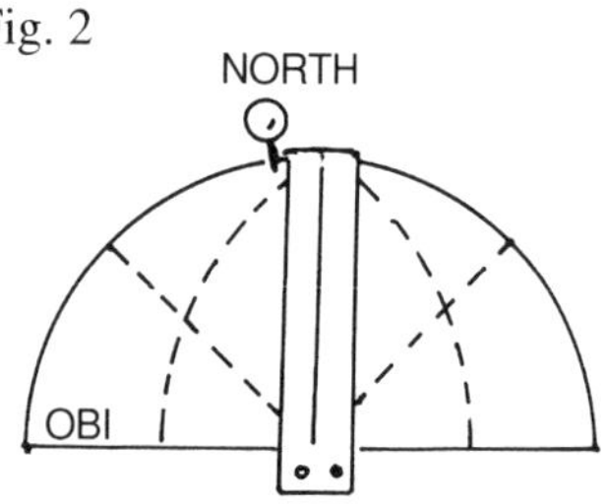

REMOVE ALL PINS except the North and South
Poles. Move the North and South Pole pins
OFF CENTER from the intersections.
They are now only direction finders.

APPLY RIBBONS:

Hold the ball with the North Pole at the Top. (Figure 2)
Start at an intersection with a Diagonal Mark.
Apply the end of Strip #1 so its end OVERLAPS
the Obi Line 1/2 inch. Pin the end with 2 straight pins.
Push pins flat into the ball.

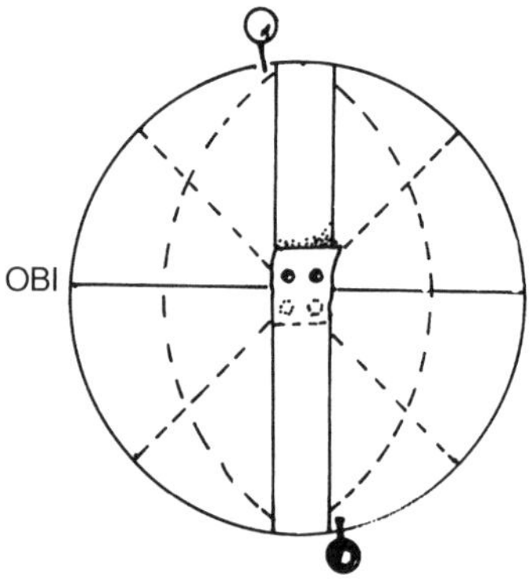

Apply the Ribbon, Centering it on the Mark Line.
Go over the North Pole, around the Ball.
End with the overlap at the Obi Line.
Pull the Ribbon TIGHTLY onto the ball.
Pin the end at the Obi Line with 2 Straight Pins.
Cut off Excess ribbon over 1/2 inch. (Figure 3)

Fig. 2

NORTH

OBI

Fig. 3

OBI

ALL STARTS and ENDS will be covered
by the Final Obi Line Wrap.

Pin the remaining 3 Ribbons to 8th Mark
Lines. Start at the Obi Line each time.
(Figure 4)

Fig. 4

NORTH

OBI

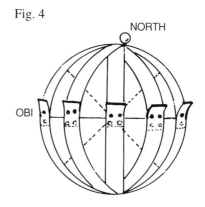

Fig. 5

OBI

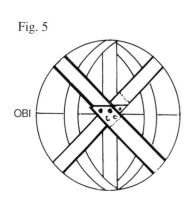

Apply 4 DIAGONAL RIBBONS to Double 8th
Mark Lines.
Begin and End at Obi Line Intersections.
Push Pins FLAT INTO BALL each time. (Figure 5)

Fig. 6

OBI LINE Start and End are hidden.
Start one end UNDER A CROSSED
DOUBLE 8TH INTERSECTION with
NO PINS. (Figure 6)

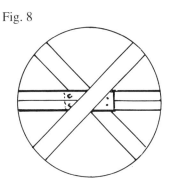

Fig. 7

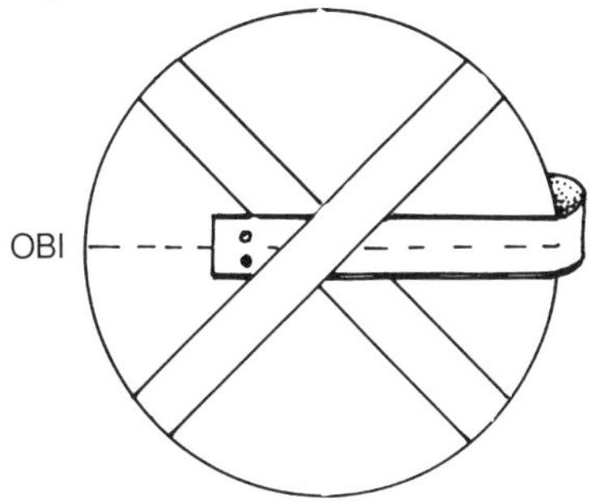

OBI

LIFT the Upper Ribbon with the Eye-end of
a needle. Slide OBI Ribbon under so 1/2 inch
end is extra at the start.
Pin with 2 Pins at the Obi Line. (Figure 7)

Fig. 8

To END, use the Eye-end of a needle to LIFT
and SLIDE FINAL OBI END UNDER
Diagonal Ribbon and Over the Beginning
Overlap. (Figure 8)

Fig. 9

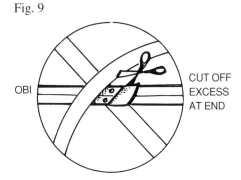

OBI

CUT OFF
EXCESS
AT END

Pull the Ribbon Tight onto the ball.
Slide the Diagonal Ribbon Over and Pin
the Obi Ribbon UNDERNEATH. (Figure 9)
Slide the Diagonal Ribbon back on top.

Fig. 10

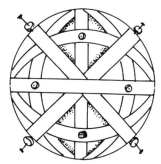

EMBELLISHMENTS
PINNED AT DIAMOND
CENTERS.

Stitch on the Lattice Pattern from "Asano-ha"
called "Antiquity" using a contrasting shade
of 1/16 inch wide metallic Ribbon.
Rhode Island Textiles metallic RibbonFloss™
Purple #18 is used here. Instructions for the
Lattice Pattern are on page 83.

The jewel embellishments are Mill Hill's
"Crystal Treasures" Margarita Topaz AB
#13007. 12 jewels are pinned inside the
Diamond Centers of the pattern.

The ball is complete.

Ball #8

"Antiquity"   ASANO-HA

Asano-ha is another of the ancient traditional temari designs, one of the oldest on record. It is a wrapped design with an over lay pattern that is stitched.

The materials replicate the very old balls made of silk threads unraveled. It is recommended that your first ball use 6-strand cotton floss. Also try overdyed or painted silk 12-strand "Waterlilies" by Caron Collection.

MATERIALS:

3 inch ball wrapped

Turquoise thread wrap:
"Waterlilies" overdyed silk 12 strand by
Caron Collection — 2 skeins "Tahiti" MA 086119
   NOTE: "Waterlilies" color number given
   is a dye lot number. Current numbers may
   differ from those listed here.

Lattice Metallic:
   Kreinik's 1/16 inch ribbon Turquoise #684

Bunka Brush ("knap raiser")

Laying tool or trolley needle

OTHER POSSIBILITIES:
ADDITIONAL COLORS and THREADS to try.

Saddle Brown thread wrap:
"Waterlilies" overdyed silk 12 strand thread
by Caron Collection 2 skeins "Navajo" JF-1117

Lattice Metallic thread — Kreinik's 1/16 inch
metallic ribbon — Copper #027

Deep Olive Green thread wrap:
DMC 6-strand Embroidery Floss — Rust #921
— 2 skeins

Lattice Metallic thread — DMC Metallic Pearl
#5 Gold #5282

Fig. 1

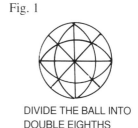

DIVIDE THE BALL INTO
DOUBLE EIGHTHS

MARK the ball:
The mark lines are meant to become invisible
when the wrapped pattern is applied. (Figure 1)

For a silk 12-strand ball:
Mark with the WRAP THREAD using an
Invisible Wrap of 3 WRAPS at each mark line.

For a DMC 6-strand floss ball,
Mark with 1 strand of cotton floss.

79

READ BEFORE YOU BEGIN:

THREAD WRAPS are PRE-MEASURED,
CUT and COMBED with the Bunka Brush
before threaded into the needle.

For the silk 12-strand "Waterlilies,"
EACH WRAP,
    measure 1 WRAP plus 6 inches.

For the DMC 6-strand cotton floss,
EACH WRAP,
    measure 2 WRAPS plus 8 inches.

Fig. 2

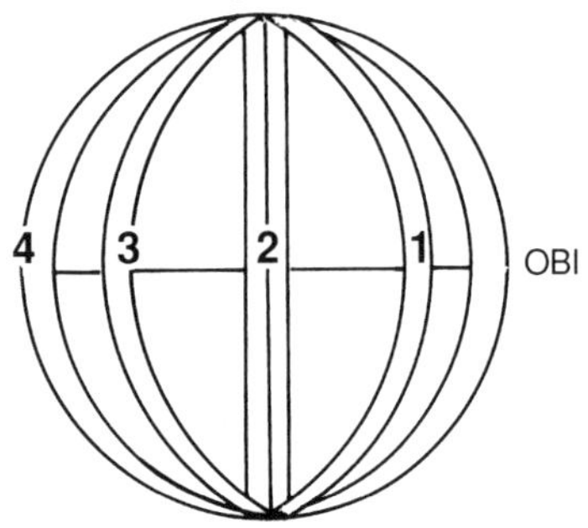

NORTH

4   3   2   1   OBI

UNTWIST and COMB the thread.
THREAD the NEEDLE. KNOT the END.

FOR EACH MARK LINE on the ball,
1/2 the wrap pattern is applied on the LEFT,
then 1/2 is applied on the right. (Figure 2)

EXAMPLE:
    1 wrap of the 12-strand silk on the left of
      the mark line, then 1 wrap on the right.
    2 wraps of 6-strand cotton floss left of the
      mark line, then 2 wraps on the right.

**ALL 8 WRAPS BEGIN AND END
AROUND THE OBI LINE.**
The final wrap is the Obi line. It covers all of
the begins/ends and disguises them.

The THREAD WRAP PATTERN is done in the
order given in Figures 2 and 3.
Follow the numbers 1 − 8.

Fig. 3

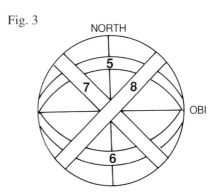

NORTH

OBI

80

Fig. 4

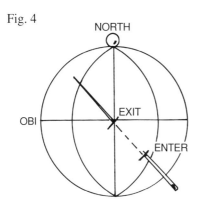

TO LAY DOWN THE WRAP THREADS:
Measure the wraps plus 8 inches extra (6 inches for silk thread). The extra makes the laying down process easier.

ENTER to EXIT at the OBI LINE. Pull thread through until the knot disappears under the surface. (Figure 4)

Comb about 4 inches with the brush. Run your needle or laying tool back and forth under the flattened strands to further flatten. (Figure 5)

Lay threads down next to the Mark Line. Run needle over the top to further flatten.

Continue to do about 4 inches at a time.

Fig. 5

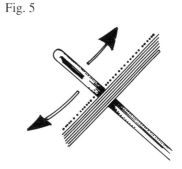

Fig. 6

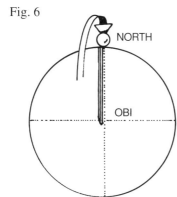

Hold the ball in your lap. WRAP in the direction AWAY from you as you turn the ball toward you.(Figure 6)

Hold the ball so you WRAP at the TOP of the ball each time.

With DMC cotton floss, wrap once next to the mark line. Align the second wrap outside the first. End where you began. Slide the threads up next to each other.

Fig. 7

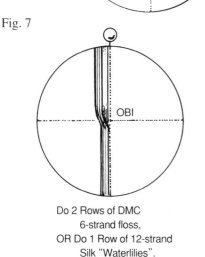

Do 2 Rows of DMC
6-strand floss,
OR Do 1 Row of 12-strand
Silk "Waterlilies".

For DMC 6-strand floss:

Fig. 8

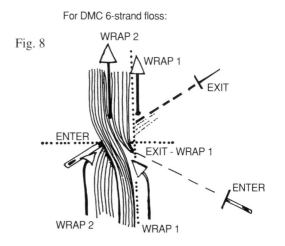

COMPLETE the 4 thread BANDS around
NORTH to SOUTH.

THE DIAGONALS:

ENTER to EXIT at the OBI LINE in the
CENTER of the band.

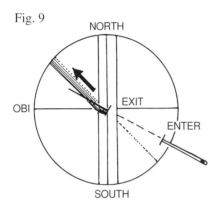

Fig. 9

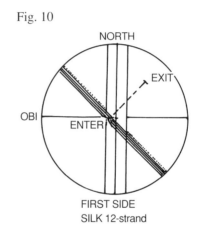

Fig. 10

FIRST SIDE
SILK 12-strand

END the wrap at the OBI LINE.
ESCAPE to the SIDE.

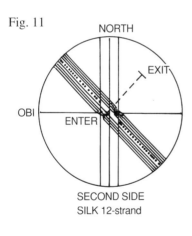

Fig. 11

SECOND SIDE
SILK 12-strand

Fig. 12

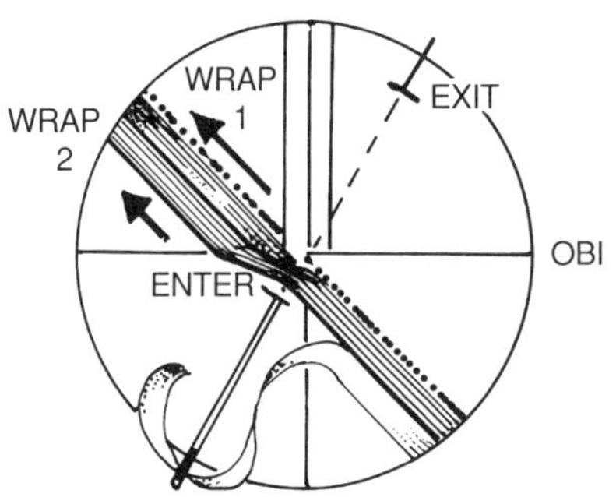

If using DMC 6-strand floss
2 Rows each side

THE LATTICE PATTERN:

Use METALLIC or CONTRASTING COLOR.
This pattern is meant to create contrast against
the wrapped pattern.

Kreinik's 1/16 Metallic Ribbons:
    Turquoise Ball — Turquoise #684
    Saddle Brown ball — Copper #027

With DMC 6 strand floss Rust #921,
use DMC Gold Metallic Pearl #5 — #5282.

Fig. 13

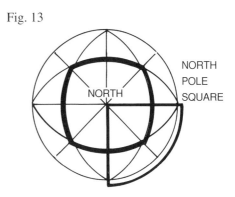

NORTH
POLE
SQUARE

Fig. 14

SQUARE:
INTERSECTION
of 4 THREADS

Fig. 15

TRIANGLE:
INTERSECTION
of 3 THREADS

Fig. 16

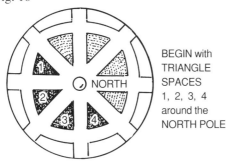

BEGIN with
TRIANGLE
SPACES
1, 2, 3, 4
around the
NORTH POLE

Thread the needle with a long length of metallic.

Follow the diagram in Figure 17.

Enter to Exit in the CENTER of the Triangle
SPACE marked number 1.

CROSS OVER the Square's CENTER
INTERSECTION of 4 threads to the
OPPOSITE SPACE in that Square.
Take a stitch — needle from Right to Left,
a regular zig zag-type stitch.
You are now in the point of a TRIANGLE.

CROSS OVER the TRIANGLE'S CENTER
INTERSECTION of 3 threads.

Look for the Square Intersection of 4 threads.
Cross through the center. Take a stitch

THE PATTERN TO REMEMBER:

CROSS OVER an Intersection of 4, THEN 3,
THEN 4, THEN 3.

Fig. 17

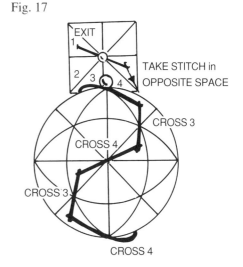

EXIT

TAKE STITCH in
OPPOSITE SPACE

CROSS 3

CROSS 4

CROSS 3

CROSS 4

The pattern row makes an Open (3-sided) Square zig zag. (Figure 18)

Fig. 18

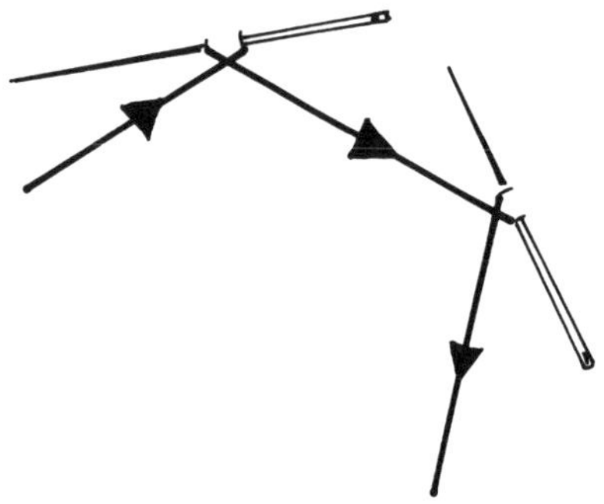

Fig. 19

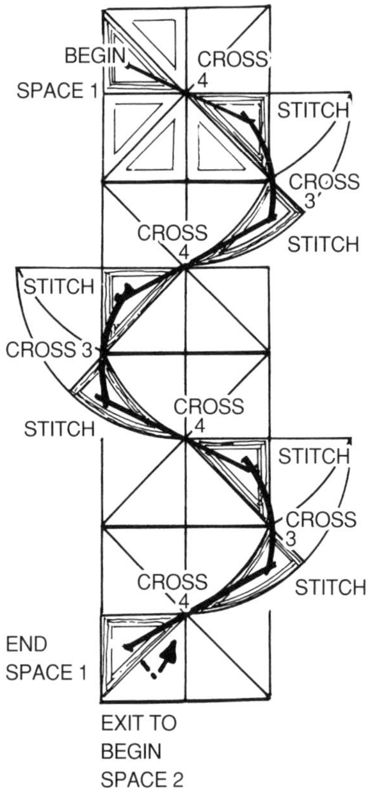

BEGIN
SPACE 1

CROSS
4

STITCH

CROSS
3'

STITCH

CROSS
4

STITCH

CROSS 3

STITCH

CROSS
4

STITCH

CROSS
3

CROSS
4

STITCH

END
SPACE 1

EXIT TO
BEGIN
SPACE 2

Continue around the ball.
You will End where you began. (Figure 19)

Complete the final stitch. ENTER, Go UNDER the surface to EXIT at the next space to the RIGHT in the Same Square. (Figure 20)

Fig. 20

END
SPACE 1
ENTER

EXIT at 2

3   4

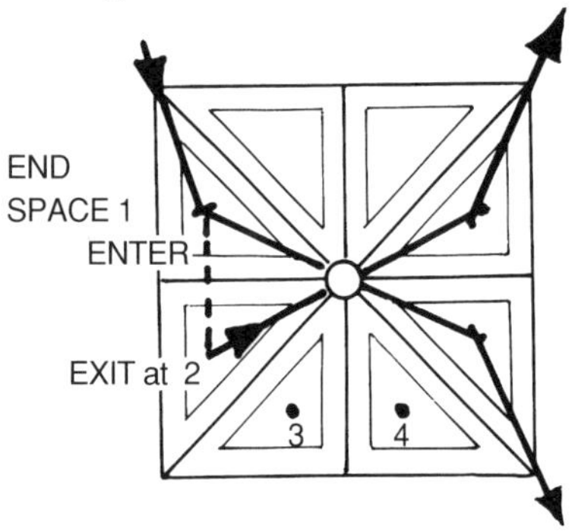

Begin again. Go around the ball.
Over an Intersection of 4, over 3, over 4, over 3.
End where you began.

Complete the final stitch. Go on to the next space in the square to the RIGHT.
Complete the row. 4 Rows start and end inside the first Square.

Fig. 21

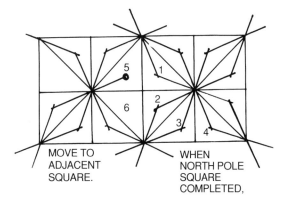

5   1

6   2

3   4

MOVE TO
ADJACENT
SQUARE.

WHEN
NORTH POLE
SQUARE
COMPLETED,

With 4 rows complete, the 8 spaces in the North Pole Square will be filled.
2 final rows remain. (Figure 21)

Move into an adjacent square with an unfilled space. Enter to Exit in the Center of the Space. Begin and end first one row around.

Then Enter to Exit at the Final unfilled space. Complete the last row around, filling the remaining spaces.

84

THE FINAL STEP:

In ALL of the DIAMOND SHAPES,

CONNECT the POINTS of the pattern
with a large CROSS STITCH across
the CENTER.

The ball is complete.

Fig. 22

Fig. 23

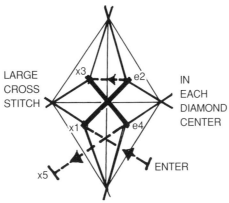

LARGE
CROSS
STITCH

IN
EACH
DIAMOND
CENTER

ENTER

85

Easy Fabric-covered Ball   **"Petals"**

A Styrofoam ball (no thread wrap) is covered with petal-shaped pieces of fabric, adhered to the ball with straight pins then with needle and sewing thread. One, two or several colors of fabric may be used.

    This design is fast and easy, with minimal stitching. Or eliminate stitching altogether by covering ends with jewelry findings or "conchas" — used for western wear, pinned to the ball. Mix bright metallic lame of gold or silver with other colors of metallic fabrics available in most fabric stores. The sparkle and color contrast makes these balls sizzle. Embellish with beads, sequins, and jewels pinned to the ball — a fast and easy finish for festive sparklers on a twinkling tree. This is a design where you'll "take the ball and run" with your own ideas!

    This ball imitates a traditional Japanese style known as *"kime komi"* in which a 3-dimensional form made of light weight wood is covered with pieced fabrics. The wooden form, in this case a ball, is incised with grooves in a pattern. Glue is pushed into the grooves. Pre-cut pieces of fabric are smoothed over the ball's surface. Edges of fabric pieces are pushed into the grooves. Sometimes gold or colored thread covers the grooves and outlines the pattern areas.

Tips

LIGHT WEIGHT cotton, silk or synthetics (men's ties from the thrift store are a good source of fabric and usually are cut on the bias) LIGHTER WEIGHT FABRIC WORKS BETTER and EASIER THAN HEAVIER (i.e. not velveteen or wool). Lighter weight fabric stretches taut. Top and bottom finish more neatly.

    Use Long stainless steel dressmakers pins not beading pins for embellishments.

MATERIALS:

3 inch Styrofoam ball (may be smaller or larger)

Fabric Scissors

Paper for pattern

1/4 yard of fabric of each selected color (s)
— Petals are cut on the BIAS of fabric.
    LIGHT WEIGHT cotton, silk or synthetics.
    (men's ties from the thrift store are a good source of fabric
    and usually are cut on the bias.)

Mill Hill's "Crystal Treasures," "Glass Treasures" and Buttons

Gold/Silver ball uses "Glass Treasures" Stars — 3 each
— #12167, 12168, 12169, 12170
Moons — 2 each — #12185, 12186
5 Gold Star Buttons — #86016
Antique Glass Red Seed Beads #03003

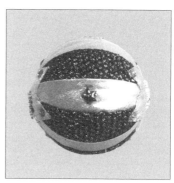

Aqua/Gold ball uses "Crystal Treasures" #13008
— 12 Blue Margaritas,
"Glass Treasures" #12040 — Large Gold Snowflakes — 2
and #12171 Dark Blue Antique Glass Large Domed Stars — 3

Dressmaker Straight pins, Colored-glass head pins

Paper measure

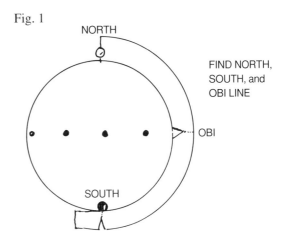

Fig. 1

NORTH

FIND NORTH,
SOUTH, and
OBI LINE

OBI

SOUTH

DIVIDE THE BALL:

On a Plain Styrofoam ball — No thread wrap,
Find the NORTH/SOUTH POLES
AND OBI with paper measure.
Mark with colored head pins. (Figure 1)

DIVIDE OBI into 4ths, then divide one 1/4
section of paper measure into 1/3s. (Figure 2)
In one quarter section only, place colored pins
around the OBI to mark the 12ths.
Use this one section as a guide to look at for
spacing the petals.

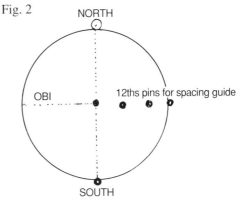

Fig. 2

NORTH

OBI

12ths pins for spacing guide

SOUTH

Fig. 3

CUT OUT THE PETALS:

Cut a paper pattern: Length = distance
North to South + 1/2 inch.
Width for 3 inch ball is 3 inches at
widest point. Scale down for smaller,
up for larger. Petals may be narrower
for adding more color panels or wider
for less. (Figures 3, 4)

Cut petals ON THE BIAS of fabric.
Place the pattern diagonally on your fabric.
CUT 12 PETALS TOTAL.
If 2 colors are used, cut 6 petals of each
color. (Figure 5)

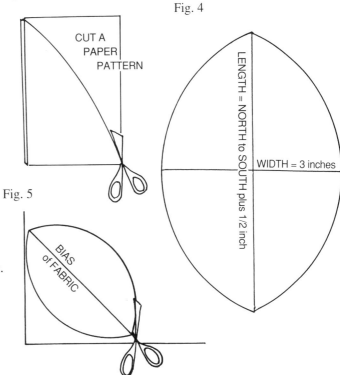

Fig. 4

CUT A
PAPER
PATTERN

LENGTH = NORTH to SOUTH plus 1/2 inch

WIDTH = 3 inches

Fig. 5

BIAS
of FABRIC

PIN PETALS TO BALL:

Fig. 6

Use the North and South Pole pins and Obi 12ths to guide you.
Look at the 12th measurement.
This will be the width of placement of each petal as it overlaps the last.

FOLD A PETAL in 1/2 LENGTHWISE (along BIAS). (Figure 6)

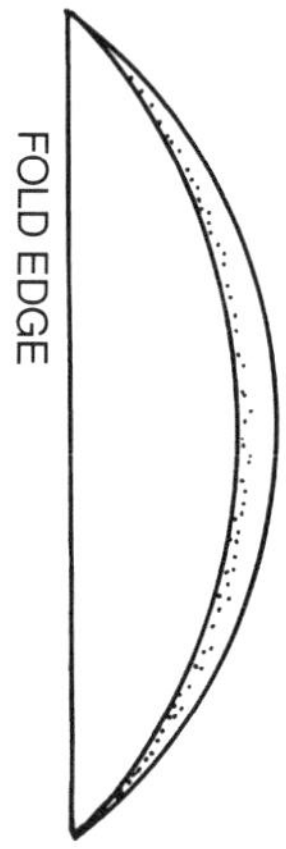

FOLD EDGE

Fig. 7

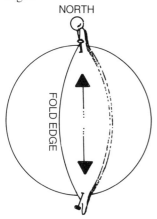

NORTH

FOLD EDGE

Pin the North Pole end 3/4 INCH OUTSIDE of the North Pole pin near the folded edge. (Figure 7)
Stretch the bias. Pull the petal TAUT, straight down the ball.

Pin the South Pole end 3/4 INCH OUTSIDE of the South Pole pin near the folded edge.
Keep the TIPS of the petals STANDING UP STRAIGHT — don't let them be pinned across the North or South Poles as you continue.

Fig. 8

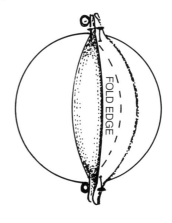

FOLD EDGE

Petal #2:
Fold petal in half. (Figure 8)
Lay it on the ball so the FOLD EDGE OVERLAPS 1/2 inch of the RAW EDGE of Petal #1 from North to South.

Pin to the ball 3/4 inch outside the North and South Poles.

Fig. 9

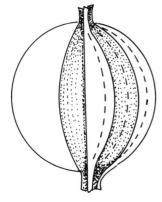

Continue around the ball,
CHECKING THE 12TH DISTANCE EACH TIME. (Figure 9)

With each Petal, Overlap the folded edge 1/2 inch over the raw edge of the last.
Lay each tip to the North and South Pole pins but pin 3/4 inch away near the folded edge.
Keep tips standing straight up.

88

Fig. 10

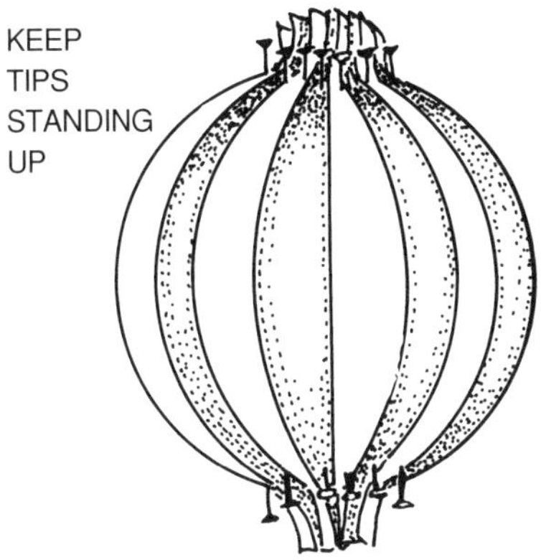

KEEP
TIPS
STANDING
UP

Stop after 6 petals and check to see that exactly
1/2 of the ball has been covered.

Pin the petal up to about 3/4 inch away from
the North Pole and 3/4 inch away from the
South Pole each time.
KEEP TIPS STANDING UP.

Continue with second half to end.
REMOVE THE 12TH MARK PINS as you go.
(Figure 10)

The final petal's raw edge is pushed under the
first petal using a dull knife or trolley needle
and then pinned in place. (Figure 11)

Fig. 11

Unpin the top and bottom of petal #1 and possibly
petal #2. Begin at the Obi Line. Slide the
RAW EDGE of the final petal carefully under
the FOLDED EDGE of Petal #1.
Work from Obi to Poles. Work tips into place
alongside their neighbors and pin back into place.

If necessary, unpin, regulate and adjust spacing
of petals. If needed, petals may be evenly spaced
by sliding out from or pushing under neighboring
panels. Do this carefully so that petal doesn't
come all the way out.

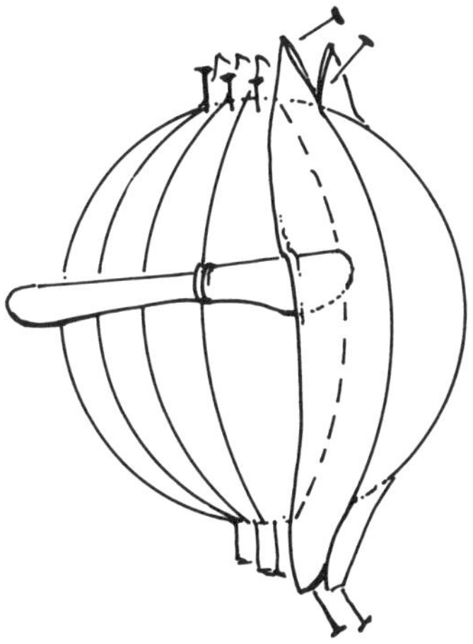

Fig. 12

BACK STITCH

BACK STITCH

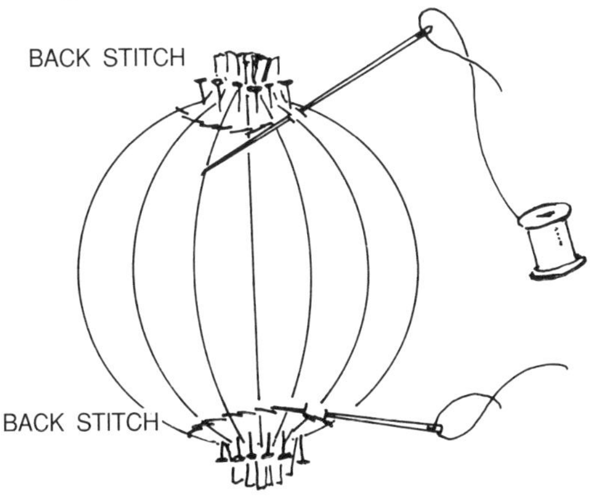

BACK STITCH with a long sharp needle
(milliner's) and sewing thread around the
North Pole, just outside the pins.
Then Remove the pins. (Figure 12)

Fig. 13

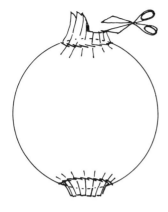

With scissors, clip the petals' tips to about 1/2 inch inside the stitching. (Figure 13)

Fig. 14

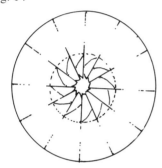

Swirl petal tips so they spiral into position and lay down flat around the North Pole Pin. (Figure 14)

Fig. 15

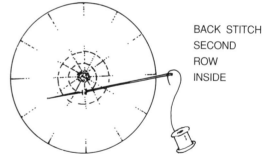

BACK STITCH
SECOND
ROW
INSIDE

Back stitch a second row INSIDE the first backstitched row. Then, across the TOP of the North Pole, do several stitches from tip to tip.
This will hold petals flat against the ball. Lock the thread.
Enter, Exit and Escape.(Figures 15, 16)

Repeat at the South Pole end.

Fig. 16

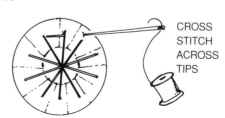

CROSS
STITCH
ACROSS
TIPS

TO COVER THE ENDS

There are 2 simple methods, CIRCLE and
STAR, to cover the stitched ends of the
balls. Both use circles of fabric.

CIRCLE: The "YO-YO," as it is known
in American quilt circles, is used here to cap
the ends with a stitched circular appliqué.

Cut a paper circle pattern 3 inches in Diameter.
Cut 2 fabric circles with the pattern.
Fold the fabric circles in half then quarters,
creasing a fold onto fabric with fingers.
This will provide a Center Mark to be used
later. (Figures 17, 18)

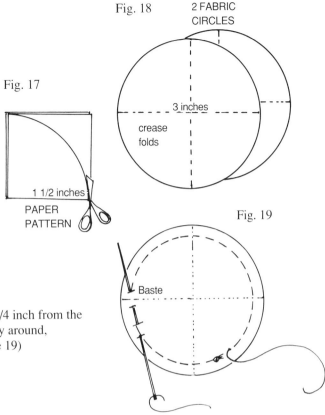

Fig. 17

Fig. 18 — 2 FABRIC CIRCLES

3 inches

crease folds

1 1/2 inches
PAPER PATTERN

Fig. 19

Baste

With sewing thread, baste 1/4 inch from the
edge of the circle all the way around,
using small stitches. (Figure 19)

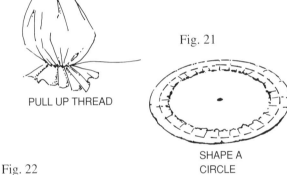

Fig. 20

PULL UP THREAD

Fig. 21

SHAPE A CIRCLE

Pull up the basting thread tight,
then loosen it as you shape the little pouch
into a flat circle. Make it as large as you
wish by letting loose the basting thread and
spacing out the stitches. Circles on the
sample ball are 1 and 1/2 inches in diameter.
(Figures 20, 21)

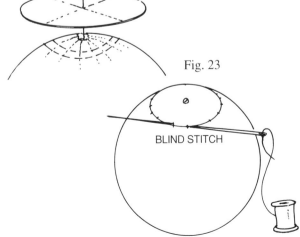

Fig. 22

Fig. 23

BLIND STITCH

Insert a Pin the fabric circle through its
folded center mark. Pin it to the North Pole.
Remove the North Pole Pin. (Figure 22)

Pin around the circle's gathered edge,
centering it onto the ball. Appliqué to the
ball with tiny Blind Stitches to cover the
stitching around the North Pole. (Figure 23)

Repeat at the South Pole end with the
second fabric circle.

91

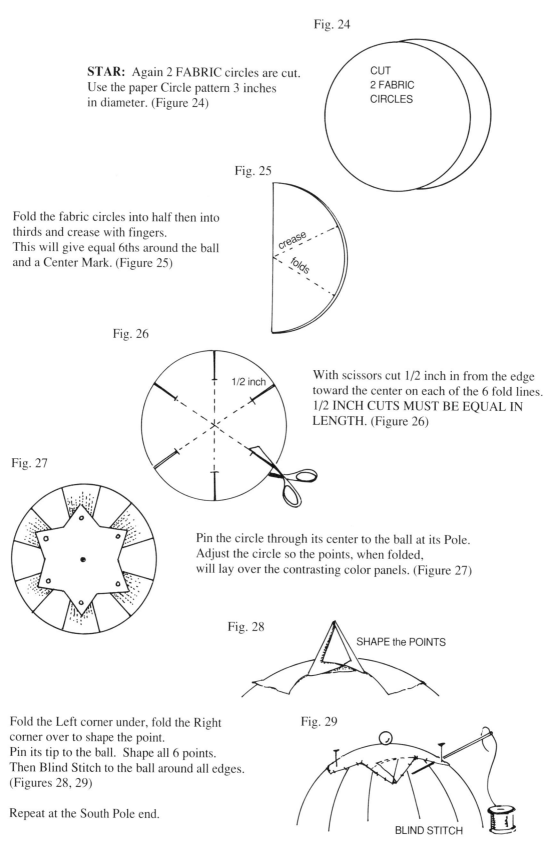

Fig. 24

STAR: Again 2 FABRIC circles are cut. Use the paper Circle pattern 3 inches in diameter. (Figure 24)

CUT
2 FABRIC
CIRCLES

Fig. 25

Fold the fabric circles into half then into thirds and crease with fingers.
This will give equal 6ths around the ball and a Center Mark. (Figure 25)

crease

folds

Fig. 26

1/2 inch

With scissors cut 1/2 inch in from the edge toward the center on each of the 6 fold lines.
1/2 INCH CUTS MUST BE EQUAL IN LENGTH. (Figure 26)

Fig. 27

Pin the circle through its center to the ball at its Pole. Adjust the circle so the points, when folded, will lay over the contrasting color panels. (Figure 27)

Fig. 28

SHAPE the POINTS

Fold the Left corner under, fold the Right corner over to shape the point.
Pin its tip to the ball. Shape all 6 points.
Then Blind Stitch to the ball around all edges. (Figures 28, 29)

Repeat at the South Pole end.

Fig. 29

BLIND STITCH

92

Fig. 30

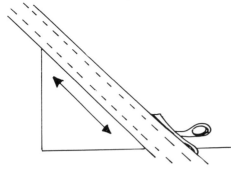

Add an Obi if you wish. Use a bias-cut strip that measures 1 Wrap plus 2 inches.
Fold the raw edges under along sides so the strip's width measures 5/8 inch.
Pin Obi to the ball. Overlap the Ends.
Turn under and Pin. Blind stitch both edges around the ball. (Figures 30, 31, 32, 33)

Fig. 31

FOLD RAW
EDGES UNDER

Use this Obi as reinforcement.
Stitch a hanging loop through the fold over ends to hang your ball so the North and South Poles are displayed front and back. (Figure 34)

Apply sequins, jewels and beads using the long dressmaker pins.
These are Mill Hill's "Crystal Treasures" and "Glass Treasures."

Fig. 32

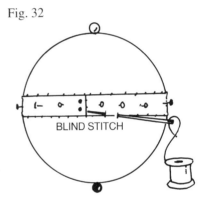

BLIND STITCH

Fig. 34

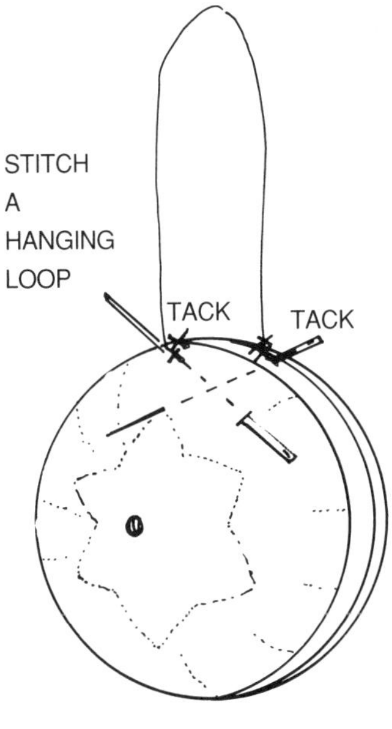

STITCH
A
HANGING
LOOP

TACK   TACK

Fig. 33

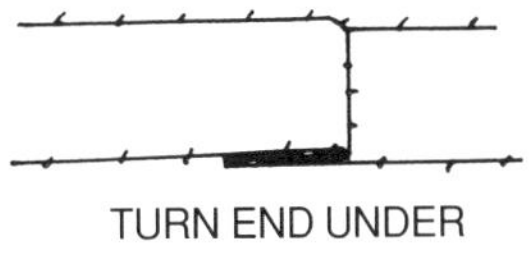

TURN END UNDER

Aqua/Gold ball uses "Crystal Treasures" #13008
— 12 Blue Margaritas, "Glass Treasures" #12040
— Large Gold snowflakes — 2
and #12171 Dark Blue Antique Glass Stars — 3.

The ball is complete.

Quilt Ball 1 **Quilt Quarters**

Another form of temari that evolved from the recycling of discards, are balls covered with pieced fabrics, new materials or salvaged pieces of favorite patterns on clothing that is well worn but too well loved to part with. Quilters will find this technique akin to their own time-honored American art form.

Quilt balls are made with simple division mark lines applied to the ball. The pattern shapes of the fabric are cut from selected division shapes on the ball's surface. Fabric is pieced together on the surface so that edges butt together along pre-applied mark lines. An abbreviated version of temari stitching covers the seams and adds another flash of contrast to the surface.

Fabrics are selected in ways similar to quilting. A limited number of colors is repeated in different proportions in chosen fabrics. Textures contrast as well as Light and Dark.

These balls, displayed as decorating accessories in a flat basket or bowl near a beloved hanging quilt, are a remarkably cooperative focal point.

In Japan, the balls are frequently made from the exquisite printed silks of the past. They incorporate memories, turn old into new. Try using photo transfers for unique mementos. Try hand or machine embroidering or couching the details before cutting the shapes out. Thin or lighter weight fabrics are preferable to flannels, velvets and woolens.

Instructions for three different division possibilities follow.

QUILT QUARTERS — Green and Gold Ball

The Beginning Ball is done from the simple division of Quarters on the ball.

MATERIALS:

3 inch Styrofoam ball

Batting, light-weight yarn and light cover of thread wrap

2 contrasting fabrics each showing the same 3 colors
— 4 scraps of each color measuring about 6 by 6 inches square

Plastic vegetable bag — clear

Permanent Marker Pen — "Sharpie"

Paper, Pencil, Foot ruler

Paper strip, Glass-headed pins

Sharp fabric shears

Needles — Sharp long Milliner's or other long fabric needle

Yarn Darner needle #18

Sewing thread to match fabrics

DMC Pearl Cotton #5 in 2 colors of the 3 in the selected fabric

94

METHOD:

WRAP the ball with batting, lightweight yarn
and a light cover of thread wrap to add fiber
to the surface of the ball. The thread wrap
smoothes out any bumps on the yarn surface.
These can cause bumps that show on the fabric
surface. Less preparation is necessary because
the surface is entirely covered with the pieced fabric.

With the paper strip and pins,
DIVIDE the ball into 4ths with an Obi Line.
(Figure 1)

MARK the 4ths with a sewing thread of
contrasting color that is easily visible.

TACK the North and South Pole
Intersections and the 4 Intersections
around the Obi Line.

MEASURE THE SIDES OF ALL
QUARTERS on the ball.
Make sure the sides of Quarters are the
SAME LENGTH ALL OVER the ball.

QUARTER MARKS on the ball make
8 Equilateral Triangles (3 Sides the same
length).

Fig. 1

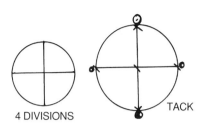

4 DIVISIONS   TACK

Fig. 2

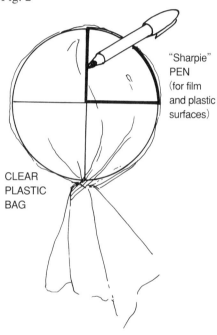

"Sharpie"
PEN
(for film
and plastic
surfaces)

CLEAR
PLASTIC
BAG

Fig. 3

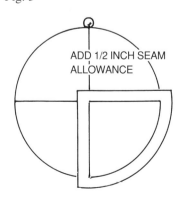

ADD 1/2 INCH SEAM
ALLOWANCE

TO CUT THE FABRIC SHAPES:

Pull a clear plastic vegetable bag over the ball.
Smooth out the creases over one entire shape of
a triangle. Make sure there are no holes in the
bag for the ink to get through. With a permanent
Marking pen like a "Sharpie," draw around the mark
lines of one triangle on the ball. (Figure 2)

Remove the ball from the plastic bag.
Smooth it out on a flat surface. Then draw another
line all the way around the triangle 1/2 inch out
from the first.
Even out the pattern so the sides are equal lengths.
(Figure 3)

CUTTING THE FABRIC SHAPES
— DON'T CUT JUST ANYWHERE!

Cut a PAPER PATTERN from the plastic
THAT IS ALSO A VIEW FINDER:
    Trace the pattern drawn on the plastic bag
    onto the paper.
    Draw the 1/2 inch OUTSIDE line of the
    triangle shape. (Figure 4)

Fig. 4

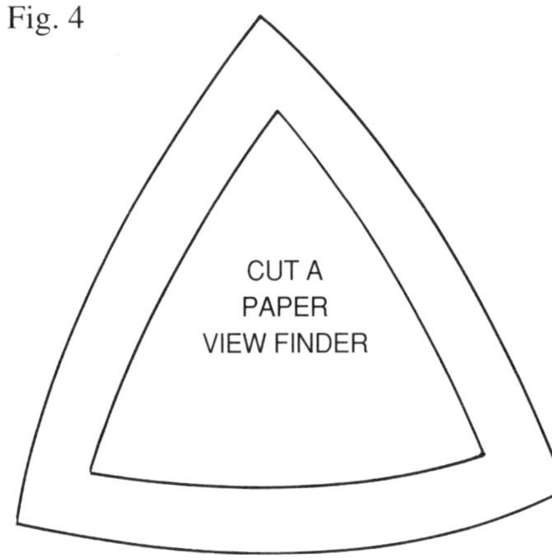

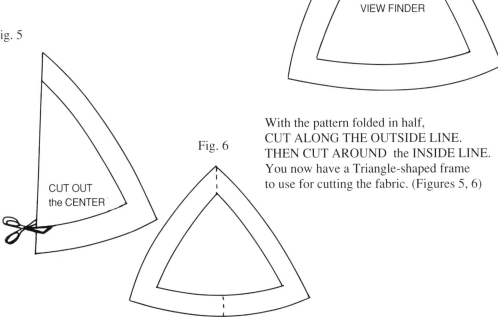

CUT A
PAPER
VIEW FINDER

Fig. 5

CUT OUT
the CENTER

Fig. 6

With the pattern folded in half,
CUT ALONG THE OUTSIDE LINE.
THEN CUT AROUND the INSIDE LINE.
You now have a Triangle-shaped frame
to use for cutting the fabric. (Figures 5, 6)

If you are using a large-patterned fabric, use the Triangle Window
to find an interesting portion of the pattern. Move the Window around
on the fabric until you select the direction and composition
(For example: it's more interesting to see the flower than the stems).
Draw around the INSIDE of the Window with chalk,
then draw around the OUTSIDE.
CUT AROUND the OUTSIDE.
The 1/2 inch width of the frame leaves
enough for seam allowances around the sides.
(Figure 7)

Cutting the fabric on the bias helps it
to lay flat on the ball's surface.

Fig. 7

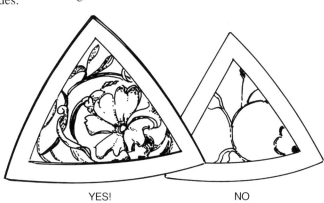

YES!   NO

Fig. 8

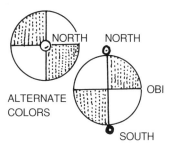

4 Equilateral Triangles (all sides of the Triangle measure the same length) will be cut from each of the two colored fabrics. The Triangles will measure approximately 4 inches on each side for a 3 inch ball.

Place 4 Triangles around the North Pole. Alternate colors. Then alternate colors at the South Pole end. (Figure 8)

Pin one triangle to the ball through the CENTER of Fabric Triangle matching to CENTER of Triangle Intersection on the ball. (Figure 9)
Adjust fabric Corners to ball Triangle Corners. Tentatively pin points into corners.

Do one corner at a time. To shape the Triangle, turn under the point first then sides on top. Fold under the POINT FIRST about 3/4 inch. (Figure 10)

Fig. 9

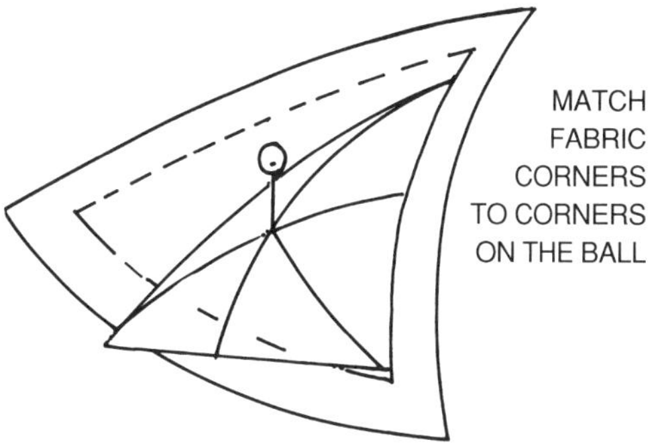

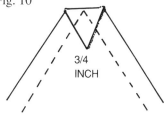

MATCH FABRIC CORNERS TO CORNERS ON THE BALL

Fig. 10

Fig. 11

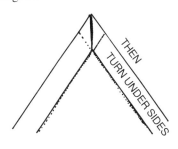

3/4 INCH

Fig. 12

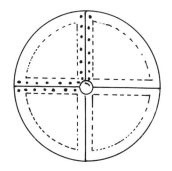

Turn under one side 1/2 inch.
Pin along the Mark line, pins about 1 inch apart.
Turn the other side under shaping the point then pinning along the Mark Line. (Figure 11)

Continue to pin on 4 triangles around the North Pole. (Figure 12)

97

Fig. 13

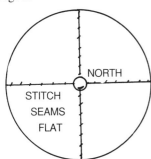

NORTH

STITCH
SEAMS
FLAT

STITCH SIDES TOGETHER with A BLIND
OR HERRINGBONE STITCH.
Use the sharp fabric needle and sewing thread.
Keep stitches small. Keep triangle sides straight.
Keep seams FLAT — NO WELT. (Figure13)
Stitches will be covered by DMC Pearl Cotton
Finishing Layer. But to do this, edges must be
flat and butt together smoothly.

Turn the ball to the South Pole end.
Pin on the 4 fabric triangles. Lay opposite
colors to those at the North Pole. Stitch sides
together. Stitch around the Obi Line. (Figure 14)
Continually use the Mark Lines to guide
placement of the triangles' edges.

Fig. 14

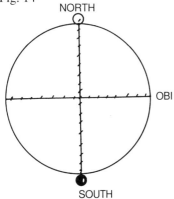

NORTH

OBI

SOUTH

Fig. 15

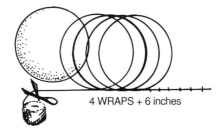

4 WRAPS + 6 inches

THE DMC PEARL COTTON BANDS:

To finish, DMC Pearl Cotton #5 is wrapped on
over the seams. 2 colors in the fabric are
used to provide contrast. Color #1 is in the
CENTER. Color #2 OUTLINES on both sides.

For the CENTER WRAP — COLOR #1,
PRE-MEASURE and CUT 4 WRAPS plus
6 INCHES. Thread your needle — DMC Yarn
Darner #18.(Figure 15)

Fig. 16

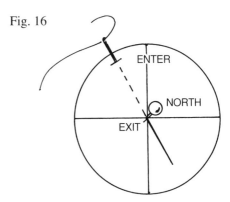

ENTER

NORTH

EXIT

Fig. 17

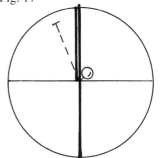

ENTER to EXIT on a SEAM that goes through
the North Pole. Pull thread through until end
disappears beneath the surface.
WRAP the 4 wraps over the seam.
Align the threads closely together over the
stitching. Back at the start on the other side
of the band, ENTER, EXIT and ESCAPE
the thread through the middle of the shape.
(Figures 16, 17)

Fig. 18   Fig. 19

For the second North/South wrap,
PRE-MEASURE and CUT 4 WRAPS
plus 6 INCHES of the SAME COLOR
thread. Wrap on.

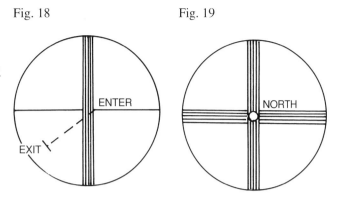

For the OBI LINE wrap, PRE-MEASURE
and CUT 4 WRAPS plus 6 INCHES,
SAME COLOR.
Wrap over the Obi Line.

Fig. 20

Fig. 21

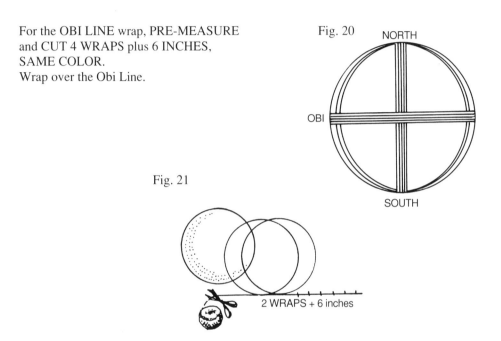

2 WRAPS + 6 inches

Fig. 22

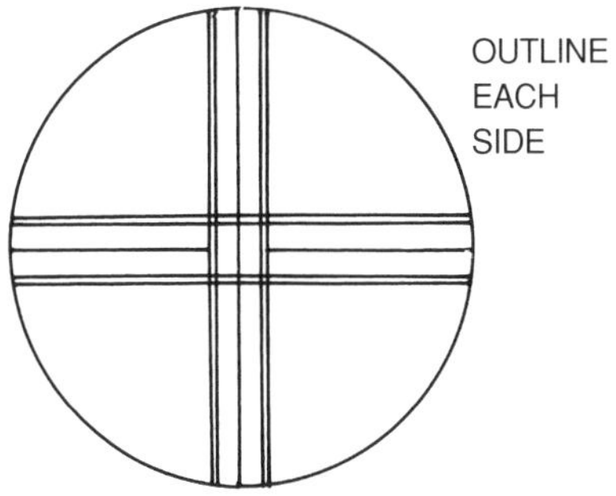

OUTLINE
EACH
SIDE

OUTLINE each band with the
SECOND THREAD COLOR. (Figures 20, 21)
PRE-MEASURE and CUT 2 WRAPS plus 6
INCHES. Wrap on the LEFT SIDE of the
first band, EXIT and ESCAPE the thread.
PRE-MEASURE and CUT 2 WRAPS plus 6
INCHES. Wrap on the RIGHT SIDE of the
first band. EXIT and ESCAPE the thread.

SECOND BAND — NORTH/SOUTH
— WRAP 2 LEFT, 2 RIGHT.

OBI LINE BAND — WRAP 2 LEFT, 2 RIGHT.

The ball is complete.

Quilt Ball 2   **Six Squares**

— Navy, Tan, and Rust

3 coordinating colors of fabrics, each with a different predominant background color, are applied on the ball like the 6 sides of a cube.

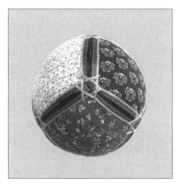

MATERIALS:

3 inch Styrofoam ball wrapped with batting, yarn wrap and thin cover of thread wrap

3 fabrics same colors within — Navy background, Tan background, Rust background

4 colors of DMC Pearl Cotton #5 in the 3 coordinating colors plus a lighter shade of one

METHOD:

DIVIDE the wrapped ball into DOUBLE EIGHTHS. (Figure 1)

MARK the ball with a contrasting thread color that is easily visible.

TACK the North and South Pole intersections and Obi Line Intersections.

TACK the TRIANGLES' CENTER INTERSECTIONS. (Figure 2)

Fig. 1

DOUBLE 8 ths
DIVISION

Fig. 2

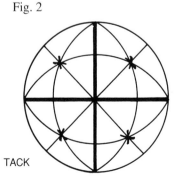

TACK

Fig. 3

CUT THE FABRIC using a pattern:
    MEASURE the SIDES of the SQUARES.
    (Figure 3)
    CUT the PATTERN with 1/2 INCH SEAM
    ALLOWANCE to turn under. (Figure 4)

Fig. 4

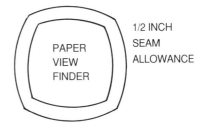

1/2 INCH
SEAM
ALLOWANCE

PAPER
VIEW
FINDER

CUT the FABRIC SQUARES:
    2 Squares each of the 3 fabric colors —
    6 total fabric squares.

PLACE the SQUARES on the ball so the colors
are OPPOSITE EACH OTHER — North/South,
Obi — front/back, Obi — right/left.

APPLY the Square to the ball with a pin in the
CENTER. Find the CENTER of the Square
by folding the Square DIAGONALLY in
2 directions to make Triangle QUARTERS.
Mark the CENTER POINT with a dot of chalk.
Place a PIN through the CENTER DOT to
the CENTER INTERSECTION of the Square
on the ball. (Figures 5, 6)

Adjust corners to corners.
Pin in place just out from center.

Fig. 5

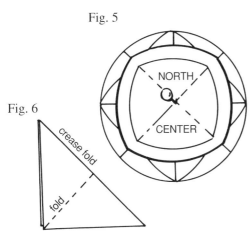

NORTH

CENTER

Fig. 6

Begin at a corner.
Fold the point under toward Center.
Fold 1/2 inch seam allowance of one side on
top then the other side at the point.
Pin one side along the Mark Line to mid-point
on the line. (Figure 7)

Then pin the other side along its mark line to
mid-point. Turn the square. Turn the point under,
then the sides. Work toward the center along
the line of each side, pinning in place about
1 inch apart. (Figure 8)

Fig. 7

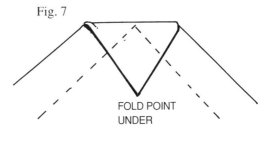

FOLD POINT
UNDER

Fig. 8

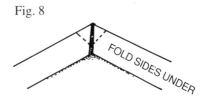

FOLD SIDES UNDER

101

Fig. 9

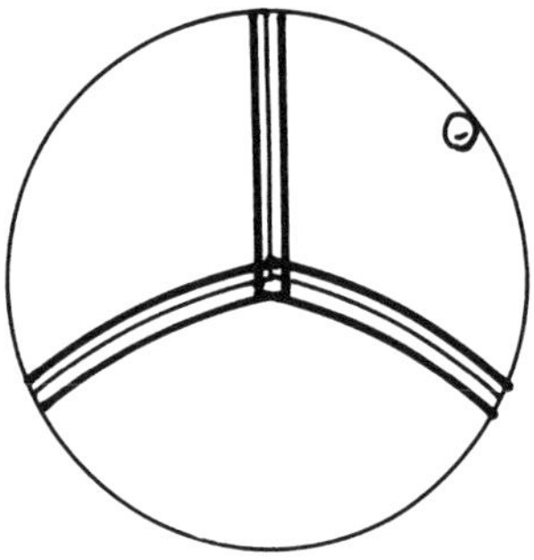

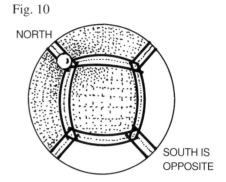

THE 3 SQUARES
INTERSECTION

When 3 Squares are pinned on, stitch their adjoining sides. Blind stitch sides BUTTED together Smoothly and accurately along ball's Mark Lines. Keep SEAMS FLAT — NO WELT. (Figure 9)

Turn the ball. Apply the final 3 Squares. Stitch sides together. The fabric cover is complete.

THE FINAL LAYER of DMC Pearl Cotton #5 COVERS SEAMS.
Thread SQUARES are STITCHED ON TOP around each Fabric Square starting from the Center outward, one row at a time.
Corners overlap.

Fig. 10

NORTH

SOUTH IS
OPPOSITE

Insert North and South Pole pins for guidance in the Middles of 2 opposite 3-point intersections. Use a RED mark pin in an Obi Square. Begin at the 3-POINT INTERSECTION at the North Pole. (Figure 10)

THREAD the #18 Yarn Darner needle with the darkest color, SINGLE THREAD.
In this example it is Navy Blue.

ENTER to EXIT in the CENTER of the 3-POINT INTERSECTION. Stitch a Square around one fabric square.
Do 1 ROW around the Square. (Figure 11)

Fig. 11

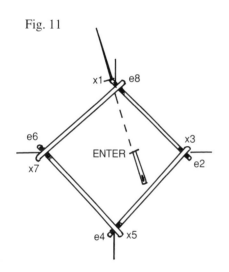

Enter the needle to finish. EXIT the needle at a corner of the adjacent Square whose point touches. (Figure 12)

Do 1 Row around Square #2.
New Rows that share the same side will lie to the LEFT of the rows around the first square.
End where you began.

ENTER TO EXIT in the corner of Square #3 and stitch 1 Row around. Exit and Escape the thread. The adjoining sides will each have 2 rows of Navy Blue.

Fig. 12

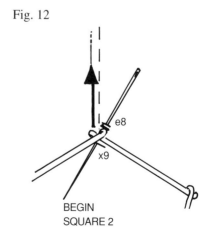

BEGIN
SQUARE 2

Turn the ball to the South Pole end,
TO THE CORNER WITH NO PATTERN
THREADS. This is your Center.
Stitch a Square of 1 Row of Navy Blue
around the 3 Squares.

TURN the Ball back to North.
DO 1 MORE ROW of Navy Blue around
each of the 3 Squares at North.

TURN the Ball back to South.
DO 1 MORE ROW of Navy Blue around
each of the 3 Squares at South.

Fig. 13

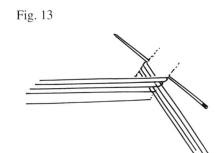

Continue to stitch 1 ROW AT A TIME
AROUND EACH SQUARE.
THIS CREATES THE CORNER PATTERN.
   TO TAKE THE STITCH AT EACH
CORNER, GO BEHIND the Rows, TAKING
a STITCH INTO THE FABRIC.(Figure 13)
   Each time a stitch is taken at a corner,
it goes OUTSIDE THE LAST and UNDER ALL
PREVIOUS ROWS. Take a WIDE STITCH
BEHIND ALL.
   DO NOT PULL CORNERS TOO
TIGHTLY or corner Star design will not lay flat.

Fig. 14

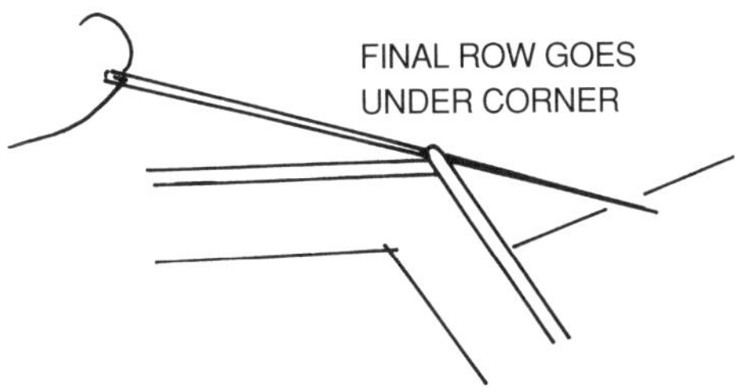

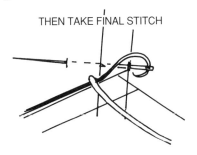

FINAL ROW GOES
UNDER CORNER

Fig. 15

THEN TAKE FINAL STITCH

The pattern continues with:
   1 Row Rust — all 6 Squares
   Second Row Rust — all 6 Squares

   1 Row Dark Teal Blue — all 6 Squares
   Second Row Dark Teal — all 6 Squares

   1 Row Light Teal Blue — all 6 Squares
   Second Row Light Teal Blue — all 6 Squares

At the Corner of each Square,
the FINAL ROW is LOCKED alongside the
previous row. Before the stitch is taken,
at all 4 corners around the final rows,
the thread is pulled under the Corner Stitch
of the row before. Then the final stitch is taken,
Enter, Exit, Escape. (Figures 14, 15)

The ball is complete.

Quilt Ball 3 **Double 8ths Offset Balls**

— Maroon & Gray, Navy & White

This Division pattern includes both Squares and Triangles in the design.
Both balls are done with 2 fabrics, same 2 colors in both but showing contrasting patterns in the fabrics.
An offset Double 8ths Mark creates the combination of Squares and Triangles.

Fig. 1

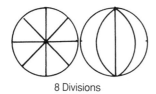

8 Divisions

Fig. 2

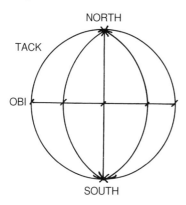

The ball is marked into 8ths around the Obi Line.
Intersections at North, South and Obi are tacked.
(Figures 1, 2)

Divide every other Mark Line in 1/2 from North to Obi and South to Obi. (Figure 3)

Fig. 3

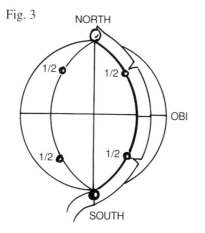

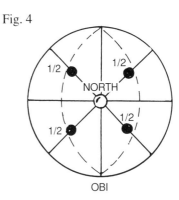

Fig. 4

Fig. 5

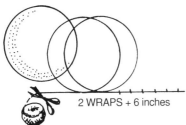

2 WRAPS + 6 inches

Fig. 6

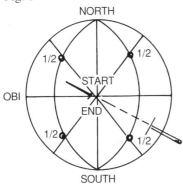

The SECOND WRAPS of the OFFSET Mark are begun at the Obi Line on a Mark Line WITHOUT A 1/2 MARK PIN. The thread is aligned along BOTH PINS as it proceeds around the ball each direction. (Figure 4)

PRE-MEASURE and CUT 2 WRAPS PLUS 6 INCHES. Thread your needle. (Figure 5)

ENTER TO EXIT at the Obi Line on an Intersection MARK LINE WITHOUT a 1/2 Mark Pin. (Figure 6)

Wrap to the Left, over the North Pole.
Align the thread along BOTH PINS to the opposite side, over the South Pole along both pins, back to the beginning. Wrap to the Right.
Complete the wrap at the Obi Line.
Tack the intersections.

PRE-MEASURE and CUT 2 MORE WRAPS PLUS 6 INCHES.
TURN the BALL 1/4 TURN to the line without 1/2 Mark Pins. Do 2 more wraps.
End where you began.
TACK the Obi Line Intersections. (Figure 7)

TACK the POINTS of the SQUARES. (Figure 8)

Fig. 7

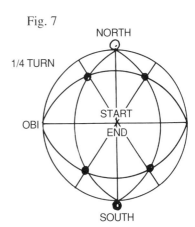

Fig. 8

SQUARES
and
TRIANGLES

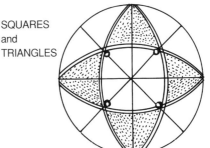

Fig. 9

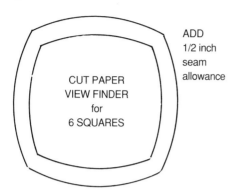

CUT the PATTERN PIECES (Figures 9, 10)
    6 Squares,
    8 Triangles.
Follow the Mark Lines. See the instructions
in the beginning of this chapter to cut patterns.
APPLY and STITCH.

The FINAL THREAD LAYER is
WRAPPED ON at the boundaries of
the shapes.

Thread Wrap Color begins in the Center.
Complete the Center Color Rows all over
the ball. Then begin the outline colors.

Fig. 10

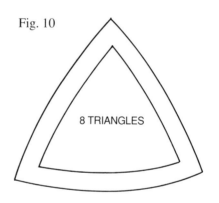

For Each Band,
Center Rows — measure 2 wraps plus 6 inches.
Outside Rows — measure 4 wraps plus 6 inches.
Wrap 2 Rows Left, go under with the needle.
Wrap 2 Rows Right. Enter, Exit and Escape.

Each side is wrapped separately.
Do Outline Rows ALL OVER the ball.

If a final row of metallic is used,
it is completed last.
Metallic rows Outline all bands.
For each thread band:
    Measure 2 wraps plus 6 inches.
    Wrap 1 Row Left.
    Go under with the needle to the other side.
    Wrap 1 Row Right.
    Enter, Exit and Escape.

Fig. 11

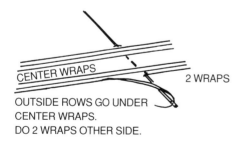

The ball is complete.

The Double 12 Mark

This division and mark will be used for both the Simple Snowflake and Traditional Snowflake patterns.

For both, a 3-inch ball is wrapped in White Sewing thread to cover the yarn wrap, then combined with Metallic machine embroidery thread #40 — Madeira White Opal color #380.

Mark Thread for both is DMC Pearl Cotton #5 White #005.

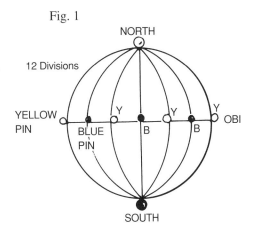

Fig. 1

LAYER 1 DIVISION

DIVIDE the ball into 12ths around an OBI LINE. (Divide the ball first into 4ths, then divide each 1/4 into 3rds.)(Figure 1)

Alternate YELLOW AND BLUE PINS TO MARK DIVISIONS AROUND THE OBI LINE.

Use the DMC Pearl Cotton #5 White #005 to MARK the 12ths around the Obi.

TACK the North and South Pole intersections. TACK the 12 Obi line intersections.

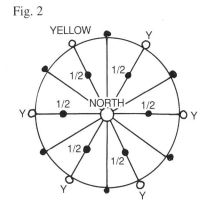

Fig. 2

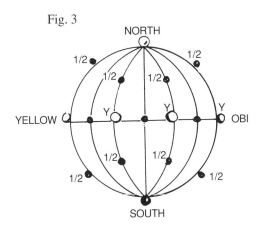

Fig. 3

LAYER 2 DIVISION

There are 6 YELLOW PIN DIVISION LINES and 6 BLUE PIN DIVISION LINES.(Figure 2)

DIVIDE the YELLOW PIN LINES in HALF from North Pole to Obi Line and South Pole to Obi Line. (Figure 3)

MEASURE and CUT White DMC #5
— 2 wraps plus 4 inches. (Figure 4)
Thread your needle.

Turn the ball so the North Pole is at the TOP and
A BLUE PIN POINTS at your NOSE. (Figure 5)

ENTER your needle to EXIT at the BLUE PIN
at the Obi.

Wrap at a 45 DEGREE ANGLE to the LEFT
and to the RIGHT just like with the Double
Eighths Wrap.
Aim toward the SECOND 1/2 MARK PIN.
The SECOND 1/2 MARK PIN is 1/4 the way
around the ball. Aim beneath the first mark pin,
go above the second, go beneath the third.

END where you began.
Tack the opposite Obi Line intersection.

Fig. 4

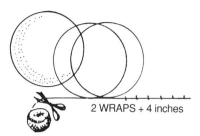

2 WRAPS + 4 inches

Fig. 5

START 1 - FIRST DIVISION

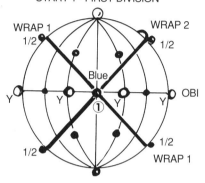

Fig. 6

START 2 - SECOND DIVISION

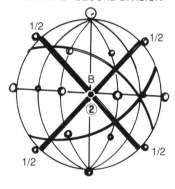

Align the mark thread *ONLY AT* the
1/2 MARK PIN at the *QUARTER
MARK*.

Align the mark thread at *ONLY ONE*
QUARTER MARK PIN.

Fig. 7
START 3 - THIRD DIVISION

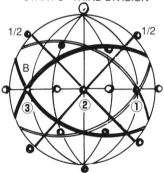

Fig. 8

At 3 BLUE PINS, complete DIAGONAL WRAPS.
At each of the 3, its opposite side will be completed.
Measure and cut 2 wraps plus 4 inches each time.
(Figures 6, 7)

This creates a "double" mark.
In effect it is a wide Obi division. (Figure 8)

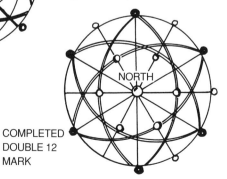

COMPLETED
DOUBLE 12
MARK

Simplified Kiku Snowflake Pattern

This pattern is derived from the traditional Aqua Blue and White Snowflake Ball, the next chapter. The pattern is similar but uses less rows and more spaces in between the rows. It uses wide ribbon to cover faster. This is a great one for Christmas gifts!

MATERIALS:

3 inch ball — wrapped in white with white opal Madeira machine embroidery thread #40 color #380

Rhode Island Textiles Metallic RibbonFloss™ in 2 colors:
    Teal Blue #15
    Deep Royal Blue #16

Rainbow Gallery's "Holo FYRE WERKS" Metallic Hologram Ribbon #FH2

Marking Thread — DMC Pearl Cotton #5 White #005

METHOD:

Use the DOUBLE 12 MARK instructions on page 107.

NOTE: When working with FLAT RIBBON, LAY it FLAT.
   To do this:
   · ENTER and EXIT needle under the mark line. Before you pull thread
   · LAY the RIBBON FLAT in LINE to where it ENTERS the ball.
   · HOLD RIBBON at the ENTRY with the THUMB of LEFT HAND to anchor as you
   · PULL thread through.

THE PATTERN:
LAYER 1

Use the RHODE ISLAND TEXTILES (RIT) Metallic Ribbon Royal Blue #16 to stitch a HEXAGON (6 POINTS) around the North Pole Pin. POINTS of the Hexagon go on lines with 1/2 MARK PINS (Yellow Pin Lines).

BEGIN Row 1 Hexagon 1/4 inch outside the North Pole Pin.

Fig. 1

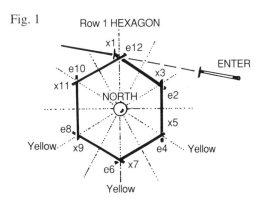

Fig. 2

Row 2 HEXAGON

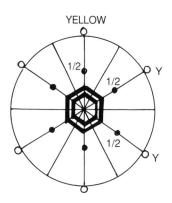

Stitch Row 2 Hexagon outside Row 1. (Figure 2)

1. KIKU Row 1 OVER the 2 Hexagons
   — Use RIT Royal Blue #16
   — Do 1 Row. (Figure 3)
   OUTSIDE POINTS of the Kiku go
   1/2 inch below Hexagon Points.
   INSIDE POINTS of the Kiku go
   INSIDE the SIDES of the Hexagon
   (near the North Pole Pin).

2. Row 2 KIKU — 1/4 inch OUTSIDE
   the last. Leave 1/4 inch space then do 1 Row
   of Royal Blue. Parallel sides by extending
   points. NOTHING OVERLAPS
   PREVIOUS ROWS.

3. Row 3 KIKU — 1/4 inch OUTSIDE
   the last. Again leave 1/4 inch space.
   Do 1 Row of Royal Blue #16.
   Again Parallel sides,
   NOTHING OVERLAPS. This time,
   OUTSIDE POINTS reach to just
   BELOW the HORIZONTAL MARK
   LINES at the 1/2 mark Pins. Inside points
   are 1/4 inch outside the previous row.

4. Row 4 KIKU — 1 Row Royal Blue,
   1/4 inch outside the last.
   Keep sides parallel.

Fig. 3

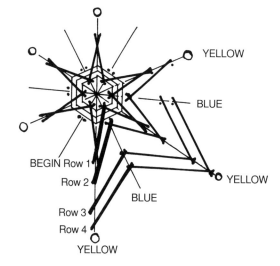

LAYER 2

OUTSIDE POINTS go below the BOTTOM POINT
of the Kite Shape on the Mark Line.(Figure 4)
OUTSIDE CORNERS go just outside the last Row
of Royal Blue #16 on the HORIZONTAL Mark Line.
INSIDE POINTS of the FIRST ROW go INSIDE
the SIDES of the Hexagon.

Fig. 4

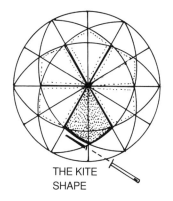

THE KITE
SHAPE

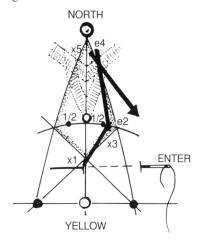

Fig. 5

ROW 1:
RIT Teal Blue #15 Metallic Ribbon
— Stitch 2 Rows of Double 12 pattern.
Begin at an OUTSIDE POINT. (Figure 5)

To keep POINTS SHAPED EVENLY
— at the RIGHT CORNER stitch,
thread is carried UNDER.
At the LEFT CORNER stitch, thread
is carried OVER. (Figures 5, 6)

Fig. 6A

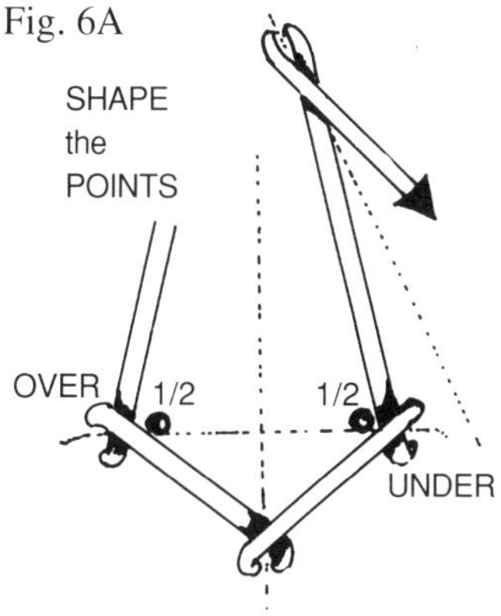

SHAPE
the
POINTS

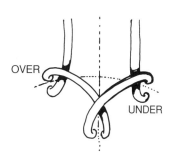

Fig. 6B

Keep CORNER and POLE
STITCHES CLOSE TOGETHER.

Keep POINT STITCHES spaced
farther apart.

Fig. 7

CONTINUE the PATTERN

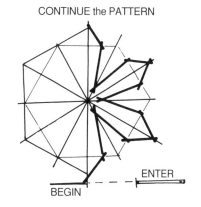

111

Fig. 8

Row 1
Row 2

ROW 2:
OUTSIDE POINTS go 1/8 inch below. (Figure 8)
OUTSIDE CORNERS go just outside the last row.
INSIDE POINTS of the SECOND ROW go just
BELOW the First Row around the Center Pole
intersection.

LAYER 3

Fig. 9

WIDE KIKU UNDER CORNERS:
6 Rows total.

Row 1:
RIT Teal #15 Metallic Ribbon.
Begin at a Point below the last Teal Outside
point. (Figure 9)
INSIDE POINTS begin in the lower Left
corner of a petal and go underneath the ball's
surface to the Exit at the lower Right Corner
of the petal on the Left.
Then aim toward the Right and take a stitch
below the next Teal Outside Point.
Continue around the ball.

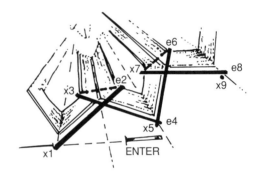

Fig. 10

Rows 2 and 3 begin just below
at an outside point. (Figure 10)

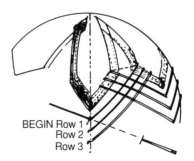

BEGIN Row 1
Row 2
Row 3

Continue the pattern with
ROW 2:
1 Row Rainbow Gallery's "FYRE WERKS"
Hologram Ribbon #FH2. (Figure 11)

ROW 3, 4, 5:
3 Rows RIT Royal Blue #16 Metallic Ribbon,

ROW 6:
1 Row Rainbow Gallery's "FYRE WERKS"
Hologram Ribbon #FH2. OUTSIDE POINTS
go just beyond (overlap) the Obi Line.

ROW 7:
1 Row RIT Royal Blue #16 Metallic Ribbon.
OUTSIDE POINTS are taken just BELOW
the Hologram Ribbon.

Turn the ball to the South Pole end.
Repeat the pattern.

Fig. 11

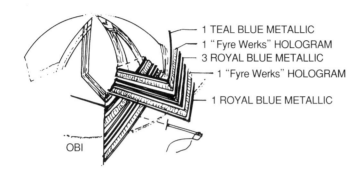

1 TEAL BLUE METALLIC
1 "Fyre Werks" HOLOGRAM
3 ROYAL BLUE METALLIC
1 "Fyre Werks" HOLOGRAM
1 ROYAL BLUE METALLIC
OBI

Fig. 12

LAST 2 Rows

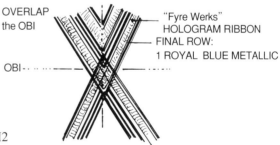

OVERLAP
the OBI

OBI

"Fyre Werks"
HOLOGRAM RIBBON
FINAL ROW:
1 ROYAL BLUE METALLIC

At the South Pole end, the final Row of
"FYRE WERKS" Hologram Ribbon #FH2
OVERLAPS THE OBI LINE.
Stitches are taken under the points of the last
"FYRE WERKS" Hologram Ribbon Row
on the North Pole side.
At the South Pole end, the Final Row is
1 Row of RIT Royal Blue #16 Metallic
Ribbon.
OUTSIDE POINTS are taken behind
the North Pole Royal Blue Points.

OPTIONAL:
Snowflake Centers at the North and South Poles
have Mill Hill's "Glass Treasures" 2 Large
Snowflakes #12039 pinned then stitched in
place with invisible nylon thread.

The ball is complete.

"Snowflakes"

This ball uses the Double 12 Division to achieve its unique pattern.
Then it uses a double-layered stitched pattern.
It is stitched with a simple pattern of larger and larger hexagons
with a variation of the Kiku Stitch on top.

MATERIALS:

3 inch ball — White thread wrap combined with metallic
machine embroidery thread #40 Madeira — White Opal #380

Marking Thread — DMC Pearl Cotton #5 White #005

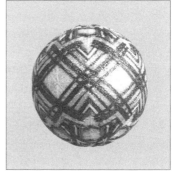

Rhode Island Textiles — RibbonFloss™ Metallic Teal Blue #15
Rainbow Gallery's "Frosty Rays" #Y209
Rainbow Gallery's "FYRE WERKS" White Opal metallic
    ribbon #F10
Rainbow Gallery's — "Fiesta" Turquoise #F735

METHOD:

Use the DOUBLE 12 MARK beginning
on page 107. (Figure 1)

Fig. 1

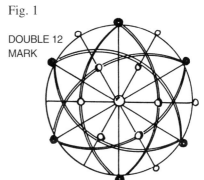

DOUBLE 12
MARK

LAYER 1 — HEXAGONS

On the *YELLOW PIN LINES:*

Use the Light Blue RAINBOW GALLERY'S
FROSTY RAYS #Y20.
Hold the ball so the North Pole points to
your nose. (Figure 2)
ENTER to EXIT AT THE TOP of the
HEXAGON, 1/2 inch (1 cm) out from the
North Pole Pin.
Stitches go around the North Pole CLOCKWISE.
TURN the ball as you stitch.
Stitch a HEXAGON using the YELLOW
PIN LINES (OR THE LINES WITH THE
1/2 MARK PINS) as your mark lines to stitch
the POINTS of the HEXAGON. (Figure 3)

Fig. 2

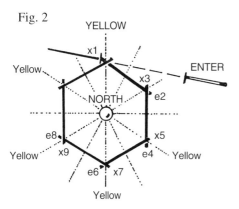

Fig. 3

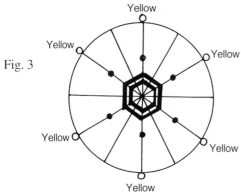

NOTE: When working with FLAT RIBBON, LAY it FLAT.
    To do this:
· ENTER and EXIT needle under the mark line. Before you pull thread
· LAY the RIBBON FLAT in LINE to where it ENTERS the ball.
· HOLD RIBBON at the ENTRY with the THUMB of LEFT HAND to anchor as you
· PULL thread through.

Do 3 ROWS of Frosty Rays #Y209 around the North Pole Pin. (Figure 4)

Do 1 ROW of RibbonFloss Teal Blue metallic #15.
Do 1 ROW of Frosty Rays #Y209.
Do 1 ROW of RibbonFloss Teal Blue metallic #15.
Do 2 ROWS of Rainbow Gallery's "FYRE WERKS" White Opal Metallic Ribbon #F10.

AT THE YELLOW 1/2 MARK PINS:

JUST INSIDE THE WHITE MARK LINE, stitch 1 ROW of Frosty Rays #Y209.
JUST OUTSIDE the mark line, stitch 1 ROW of RibbonFloss Teal Blue #15.

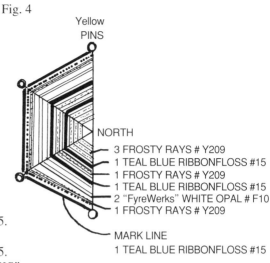

Fig. 4

Yellow
PINS

NORTH

3 FROSTY RAYS # Y209
1 TEAL BLUE RIBBONFLOSS #15
1 FROSTY RAYS # Y209
1 TEAL BLUE RIBBONFLOSS #15
2 "FyreWerks" WHITE OPAL # F10
1 FROSTY RAYS # Y209

MARK LINE
1 TEAL BLUE RIBBONFLOSS #15

LAYER 2 — THE SNOWFLAKE PATTERN

MARK THE PATTERN:

Around each yellow pin, the mark lines form a KITE-SHAPE. (Figure 5)
DIVIDE the HORIZONTAL LINE in HALF ON EITHER SIDE OF THE YELLOW 1/2 Mark PIN.
Remove the Yellow 1/2 mark pins at Hexagon Points.
Replace them as Line Markers at the Obi line for use at the South Pole end. (Figure 6)

Thread needle with a long length of Rainbow Galleries — "Fiesta" Turquoise #F136.

Fig. 5

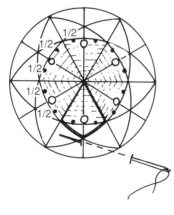

Fig. 6

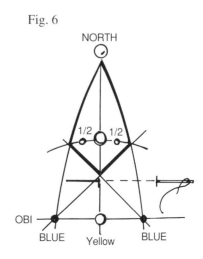

NORTH

OBI

BLUE   Yellow   BLUE

Fig. 7

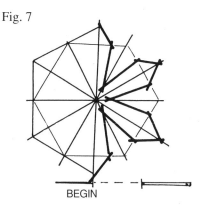

BEGIN

Use the KIKU Stitch. The stitch is taken at the BOTTOM of the pattern and goes COUNTER CLOCKWISE. (Figure 7)

ENTER to EXIT just BELOW and to the LEFT of the KITE'S POINT on a YELLOW PIN LINE.

FIRST ROW: Stitch INSIDE STITCHES CLOSE to the POLE on the Mark Line. As you take each corner stitch, REMOVE the PIN.

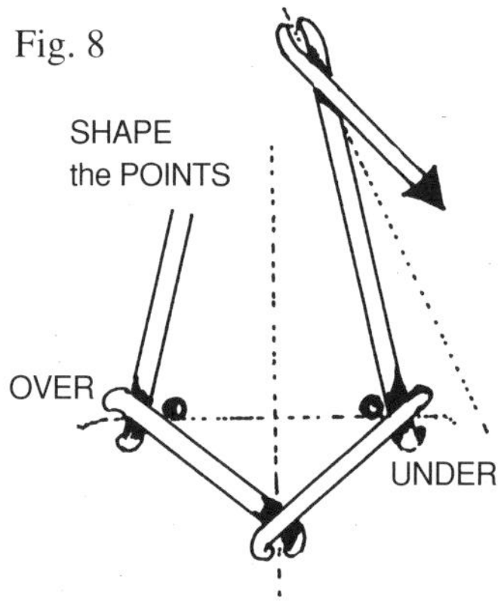

To keep POINTS SHAPED EVENLY — at the RIGHT CORNER stitch, thread is carried UNDER. At the LEFT CORNER stitch, thread is carried OVER.(Figures 8, 9)

Keep CORNER and POLE STITCHES CLOSE TOGETHER.

Keep POINT STITCHES spaced farther apart.

Fig. 8

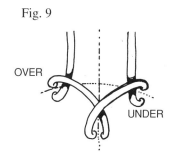

SHAPE the POINTS

OVER

UNDER

Fig. 9

OVER

UNDER

Do 2 ROWS Rainbow Galleries "Fiesta" TEAL BLUE #F735. DO NOT ATTEMPT TO LAY THIS FLAT.

Do 1 ROW RibbonFloss Metallic Teal Blue #15. BEGIN again at an OUTSIDE POINT (Kite Point). Inside point stitches ENTER ABOVE the FIRST Teal ROW of the HEXAGON.

With DMC Pearl Cotton #5 White #005, use a DOUBLE THREAD. BEGIN at an OUTSIDE POINT.
   Do 1 ROW (2 threads. Lay threads flat. Miter corners).
   Enter INSIDE POINT (Pole) Stitches just BELOW First Teal Blue Row of the Hexagon.

With RibbonFloss Metallic Teal Blue #15, do 2 ROWS outside the White DMC.
   Row 1 INSIDE Stitches enter BELOW HEXAGON ROW 5 — Frosty Rays.
   Row 2 INSIDE Stitches enter BELOW HEXAGON ROW 6 — Teal Blue metallic (second row).

Fig. 10

THE STAR PATTERN

116

Fig. 11

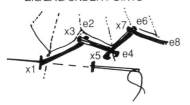

ZIG ZAG UNDER POINTS

ZIG ZAG 1 ROW:

With "FYRE WERKS" White Opal Ribbon #F10,
do 1 ROW of ZIG ZAG stitch BELOW the points
of the Snowflake and UP into the CORNERS.
Follow the diagram. (Figures 11,12)

Fig. 12

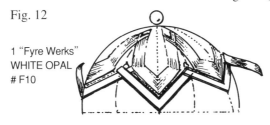

1 "Fyre Werks"
WHITE OPAL
F10

KIKU UNDER CORNERS

With RibbonFloss Metallic Teal Blue #15,
do 1 ROW of Kiku Stitch.
ENTER to EXIT at a POINT, just BELOW
the 1 White Opal Zig Zag row. (Figure 13)
Next enter at a CORNER, go UNDER
the entire width of the threads,
EXIT at the CORNER to the LEFT.
Go on to the Point at RIGHT, take a stitch.

Fig. 13

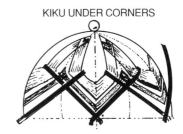

KIKU UNDER CORNERS

ROW 2 is "FYRE WERKS" White Opal
Ribbon #F10, OUTSIDE ROW 1. (Figure 14)

ROWS 3 and 4, Teal Blue Metallic RibbonFloss
#15 is stitched JUST OUTSIDE row 2.
Do 2 ROWS. (Figure 14)

Fig. 14

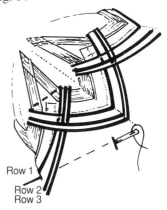

Row 1
Row 2
Row 3

Fig. 15

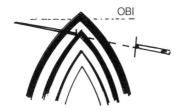

OBI

POINTS may OVER LAP the Obi Line slightly.
(Figure 15)

REPEAT the pattern at the South Pole.

THE OBI is completed with 2 final Zig Zag rows of RIT Teal Blue Metallic Ribbon #15. Points overlap at the Obi Line into the second rows of RIT Teal Blue Metallic Ribbon #15.

Fig. 16

KIKU UNDER CORNERS is SPACED AWAY 1/4 INCH so that the Zig Zag follows the original lines of the design. (Figure 16)

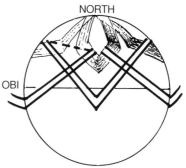

Turn the ball, North Pole to TOP. ENTER to EXIT AT A POINT in the SECOND BLUE TEAL ROW on the SOUTH POLE Pattern.

Kiku Under Corners of the North Pole Pattern. SPACE the stitch to ENTER 1/4 INCH BEFORE the previous 2 rows of Teal Blue and EXIT 1/4 INCH PAST them. The Line of the new row FOLLOWS the SAME DIRECTION as previous rows. Complete the North Pole Kiku.

Fig. 17

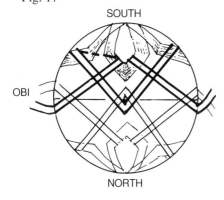

Turn the South Pole to TOP. Complete the South Pole pattern. (Figure 17)

The ball is complete.

118

The Pentagons Mark

Pentagons
Mark Symbol

Fig. 1

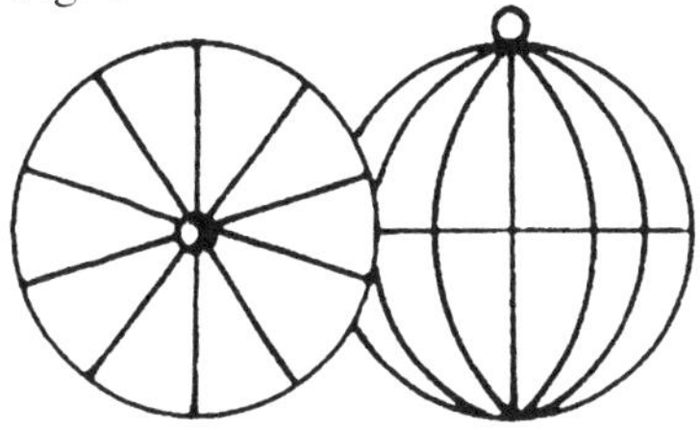

Divide into 10ths around OBI.

Fig. 2

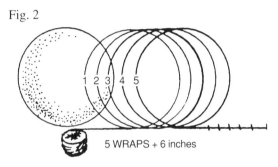

5 WRAPS + 6 inches

MEASURE 5 WRAPS plus 6 inches of marking thread.

Fig. 3

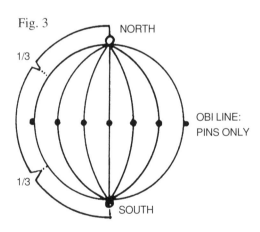

NORTH

1/3

OBI LINE:
PINS ONLY

1/3

SOUTH

MARK the 10ths with thread.

DO NOT MARK THE OBI LINE WITH THREAD.
Use pins only.
DIVIDE into 1/3s between NORTH and SOUTH POLES.

Fig. 4

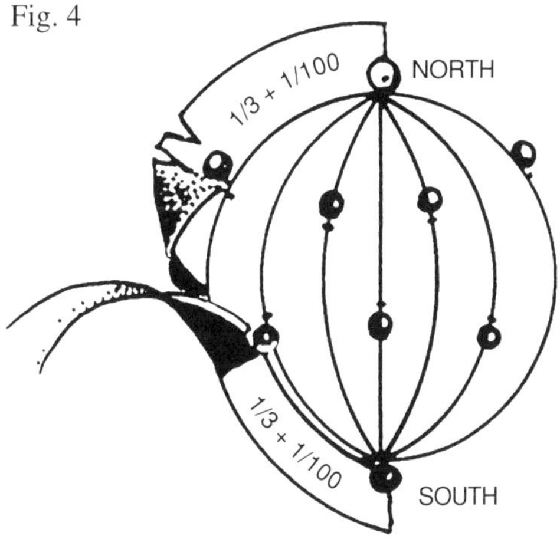

1/3 + 1/100

NORTH

1/3 + 1/100

SOUTH

WITH PINS, mark upper 1/3 and lower 1/3 on alternating lines.
ADD 1/100 of the circumference more to EACH 1/3 toward the OBI LINE.
(✳ see NOTE below.)

✳ NOTE : The 1/100 measurement is found by measuring the total distance around the ball (circumference) with your centimeter tape. Divide the total by 100. This extra added bit (about 1/8 inch or 3 millimeters on a 4-inch ball) to each 1/3 makes the pentagon divisions more accurate. Don't ask me why.

Fig. 5

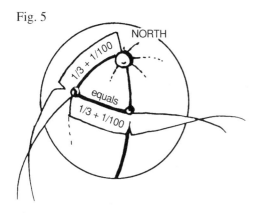

1/3 measurements are EQUAL IN ALL
DIRECTIONS. CHECK them for accuracy.

Fig. 6

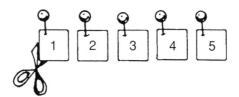

CUT 10 PAPER tabs.
MARK the UPPER 1/3s with NUMBERS.

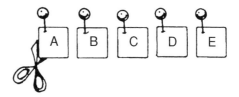

MARK the LOWER 1/3s with LETTERS.

Fig. 7

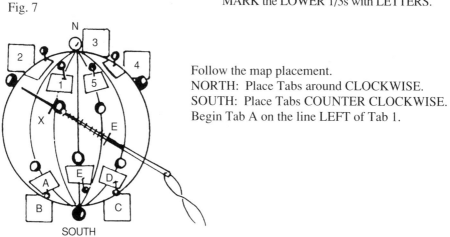

Follow the map placement.
NORTH: Place Tabs around CLOCKWISE.
SOUTH: Place Tabs COUNTER CLOCKWISE.
Begin Tab A on the line LEFT of Tab 1.

Fig. 8

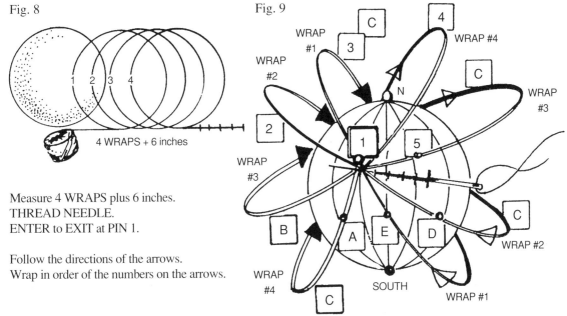

4 WRAPS + 6 inches

Measure 4 WRAPS plus 6 inches.
THREAD NEEDLE.
ENTER to EXIT at PIN 1.

Follow the directions of the arrows.
Wrap in order of the numbers on the arrows.

Fig. 9

Follow WRAP NUMBER 1 from PIN #1,
around the ball to 3, to C, to E, back to 1.
WRAP NUMBER 2: 1 — 2 — C — D — 1
WRAP NUMBER 3: 1 — B — C — 5 — 1
WRAP NUMBER 4: 1 — A — C — 4 — 1
ESCAPE.
DO NOT TACK YET.

Fig. 10

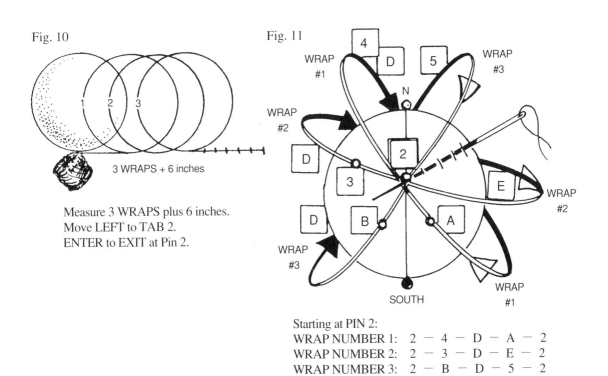

3 WRAPS + 6 inches

Measure 3 WRAPS plus 6 inches.
Move LEFT to TAB 2.
ENTER to EXIT at Pin 2.

Fig. 11

Starting at PIN 2:
WRAP NUMBER 1: 2 — 4 — D — A — 2
WRAP NUMBER 2: 2 — 3 — D — E — 2
WRAP NUMBER 3: 2 — B — D — 5 — 2
ESCAPE, DO NOT TACK YET.

Fig. 12

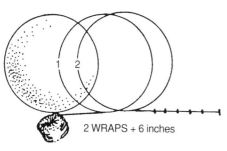

2 WRAPS + 6 inches

Measure 2 WRAPS plus 6 inches.

Fig. 13

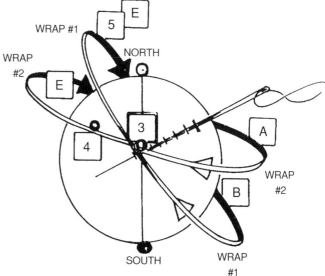

ENTER to EXIT at PIN 3.

WRAP NUMBER 1: 3 — 5 — E — B — 3
WRAP NUMBER 2: 3 — 4 — E — A — 3
ESCAPE, DO NOT TACK.

Fig. 14

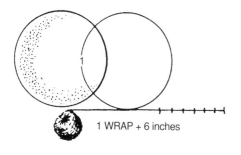

1 WRAP + 6 inches

Measure 1 WRAP plus 6 inches.

Fig. 15

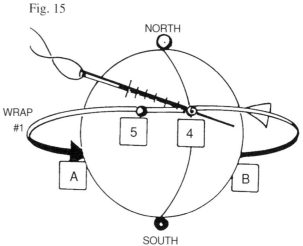

ENTER to EXIT at PIN 4.

FINAL WRAP TO COMPLETE:
        4 — 5 — A — B — 4.

BEFORE YOU TACK:

ADJUST THREADS to make regular shapes.
CHECK PENTAGON CENTERS.
CHECK TRIANGLE CENTERS.

ADJUST LINES.
TACK ALL 12 Pentagon Centers.

The mark is complete.

Ball #15
Multi-colored Stars on Pentagons   **"Halo Stars"**

Six different bright colored stars are backed by pentagons of their corresponding pastel colors.
This is a wonderful display of color using a very simple and fast pattern.

MATERIALS:

3 inch ball — Dark forest green thread wrap

12 colors of DMC Pearl Cotton #5, 6 Pastel shades,
6 Deep shades

1. RED Light #3081
   RED Deep #666
2. GREEN Light #959
   GREEN Deep #991
3. PURPLE Light #553
   PURPLE Deep #550
4. YELLOW Light #725
   YELLOW Deep #972
5. BLUE Light #798
   BLUE Deep #820
6. ORANGE Light #970
   ORANGE Deep #900

GOLD Metallic Marking Thread
— Kreinik Balger Ombre Gold #2000
or Fine Braid #8 color #002,
or Y.L.I. "Candlelight" Gold

Fig. 1

PENTAGONS
DIVISION

METHOD:

DIVIDE the ball into PENTAGONS.
MARK the ball with the GOLD metallic mark thread. (Figure 1)

    TACK the PENTAGON CENTERS and
    TRIANGLE CENTERS. (Figure 2)

    The pattern is developed in 2 layers within
    each pentagon mark:
        Layer 1 — pastel pentagon
        Layer 2 — bright star.
    Gold metallic outlines the inside and outside
    of each layer.

    Each of the 6 pentagons around the North Pole
    displays a different color.
    That Color is repeated in the opposite pentagon
    at the South Pole end.

Fig. 2

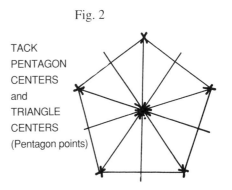

TACK
PENTAGON
CENTERS
and
TRIANGLE
CENTERS
(Pentagon points)

123

LAYER 1 — PASTEL PENTAGONS:

Fig. 3

Begin at the North Pole with Gold and Light Red #3081. (Figure 3)

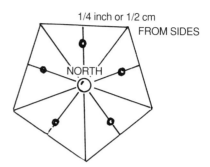

Measure the SHORT LINES — the LINES to the SIDES of the pentagon, 1/4 inch or 1/2 cm in from the sides and mark with pins. Thread your needle with Gold mark thread. Knot the thread's end. Enter to Exit at the TOP SIDE of the pentagon.

Fig. 4

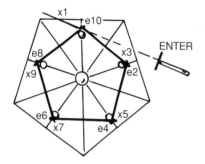

The Pastel Pentagons are stitched starting the TOP of the pattern.
Turn the pattern COUNTER CLOCKWISE as you take each stitch so the stitch is taken at the TOP EACH TIME. (Figure 4)

Stitch 1 Row of Gold metallic around the 1/4 inch (1/2 cm) mark pins. (Figure 5)

Fig. 5

NOTE WHEN STITCHING:

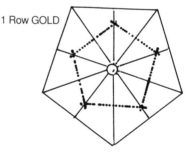

The INSIDE GOLD ROWS
can be applied all over the ball,
then PASTEL Rows all over the ball,
then outline Gold Rows all over the ball,
before going on to Layer 2 Stars.
OR one entire pattern of both layers
may be completed at a time.

Fig. 6

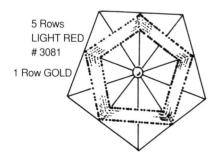

Outside the Gold,
stitch 5 Rows of Light Red #3081
DMC Pearl Cotton. (Figure 6)
Stitch 1 Row of Gold around
the 5 Light Red rows.

Follow the map to place colors on the ball.
Place the same color at the opposite
pentagon at the South Pole end.

Fig. 7

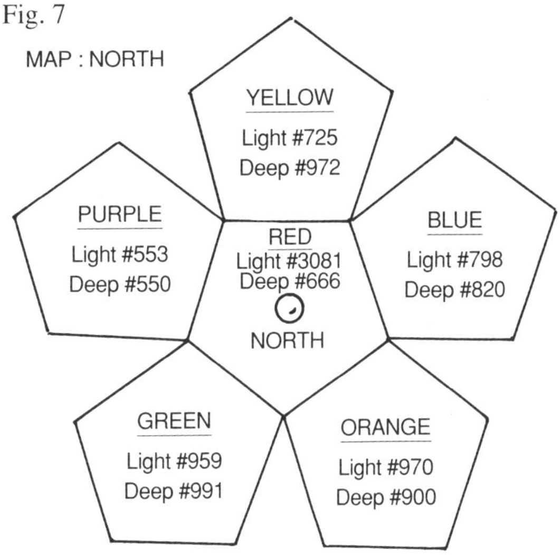

MAP : NORTH

YELLOW
Light #725
Deep #972

PURPLE
Light #553
Deep #550

RED
Light #3081
Deep #666

NORTH

BLUE
Light #798
Deep #820

GREEN
Light #959
Deep #991

ORANGE
Light #970
Deep #900

Fig. 8

BRIGHT STARS

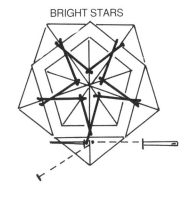

Fig. 9

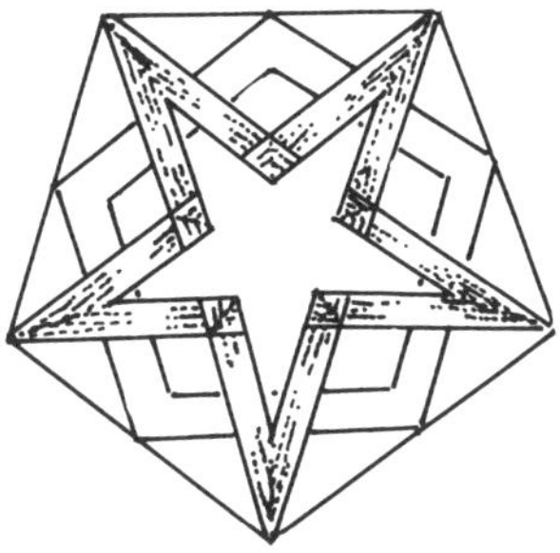

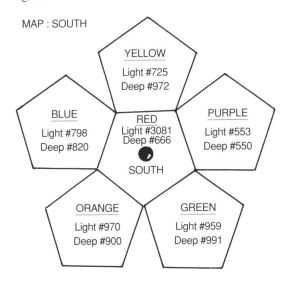

Fig. 10

MAP : SOUTH

YELLOW
Light #725
Deep #972

BLUE
Light #798
Deep #820

RED
Light #3081
Deep #666

SOUTH

PURPLE
Light #553
Deep #550

ORANGE
Light #970
Deep #900

GREEN
Light #959
Deep #991

LAYER 2 — BRIGHT STARS:

KIKU Stitch is used for the star.
The Kiku Stitch begins at the BOTTOM of
the pattern. The stitches go in a Zig Zag
around the center COUNTER CLOCKWISE.
(Figure 8)

Star POINTS BEGIN just BELOW
Pastel Pentagon SIDES.
Star Points EXTEND to TOUCH
Pentagon POINTS. (Figure 9)
Star INSIDE POINTS' stitches are taken
just outside the Center of the Pentagon.

1 Row Gold,
4 Rows Deep Color,
1 Row Gold.

Complete the two layers of pattern in
all 12 pentagons, North and South.

The ball is complete.

125

Pentagons Overlap   "Rings on Quiet Water"

This is a perfect ball to display with your favorite quilt balls. Its pattern mimics the intricate pieced pattern of a quilt. Repeat 6 colors of your favorite quilt. Select 6 colors that all work together because they will all touch each other.

    The pattern uses the boundary lines of the 12 pentagons. One row is applied around all 12 pentagons creating one layer. Successive layers fill in the surrounding pentagons toward their centers. Centers are filled in later using colors that correspond with the boundary colors.

MATERIALS:

2 1/2 or 3 inch ball — Royal Purple thread wrap

6 colors of DMC Pearl Cotton #5
    Yellow #741
    Orange # 947
    Red #666
    Magenta #915
    Blue #820
    Aqua #995

Fig. 1

Metallic Gold Mark thread
    Kreinik Balger Ombre #2000 or
    Y L I "Candlelight" Gold

Paper Tabs — 12 — 2 sets numbered 1 to 6

PENTAGONS
DIVISION

METHOD:

Fig. 2   TACK

DIVIDE the ball into pentagons.
Mark with metallic gold. (Figure 1)

PENTAGON
CENTERS
and
POINTS

TACK the Pentagon Centers. (Figure 2)

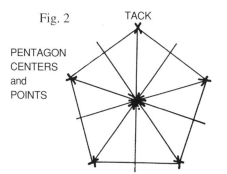

TACK the Triangle Centers (Pentagons' points) so Mark thread positions are secure.

Fig. 3

CUT PAPER TABS

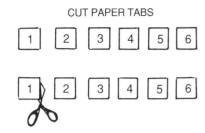

Fig. 4

MAP : NORTH

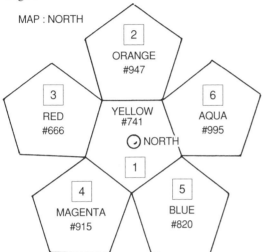

BEGIN WITH the NORTH POLE PENTAGON.
Enter to Exit outside the pentagon boundary line,
just above and to the left of a line "to a point."
The first row will go around the outside of the
pentagon mark, USE THE VERTICAL LINE OF
THE POINTS EACH TIME TO TAKE THE
STITCH. (Figure 5)

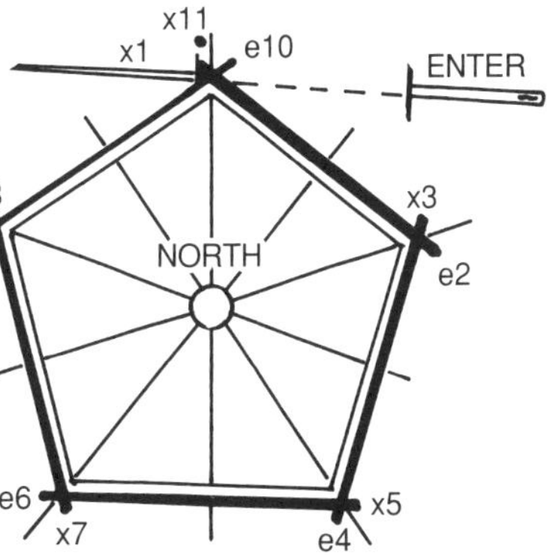

Do 1 Row around the North Pole pentagon.

With each pentagon a different color,
Go on to pentagons 2, 3, 4, 5 and 6 and then to
their opposites at the South Pole end on the ball.
When all 12 pentagons have 1 Row,
this completes Layer #1. (Figure 6)

Use a MARK PIN of a different color to mark
your place when you stop.

THE THREAD PATTERN:

The boundaries of all 12 pentagons begin
the first rows of pattern threads.
The pattern is applied, 1 Row of each color,
around the outside of each pentagon mark line.

There are 6 Pentagons around the North Pole
and 6 pentagons around the South Pole.
Rows are applied following the order of the
numbered markers 1 through 6, first around
the North Pole, then 1 through 6 around the
South Pole.

NUMBER THE PENTAGONS 1 THROUGH 6
around the North Pole with paper dots.
Number the pentagons 1 THROUGH 6 around
the South Pole SO THE COLORS ARE
OPPOSITE ON THE BALL.

Fig. 5

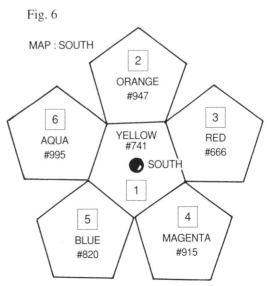

Fig. 6

MAP : SOUTH

Fig. 7

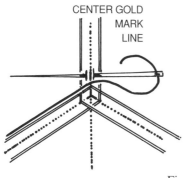

CENTER GOLD
MARK
LINE

Start again at the North Pole with Layer 2.
Apply 1 row at all 12 Pentagons,
IN the SAME ORDER — 1 THROUGH 6 NORTH
and 1 through 6 SOUTH.

For Row 2 and continuing rows,
the stitches are taken up the Center Gold Mark Line
by separating the threads along each side. (Figure 7)
TAKE the STITCH UNDER the GOLD MARK LINE
ONLY, DO NOT CATCH COLORED THREAD
ROWS in the stitch — GO OVER THEM.

Fig. 8

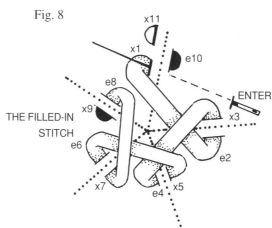

THE FILLED-IN
STITCH

The CENTERS of each pentagon may be stitched
with 3 to 4 Rows of the Boundary color to remind
of the color used. See Filled-in Stitch Figure 8.

Fig. 9

The Centers will be filled in from the Center
Intersection outward with the fill-in (Spiderweb
inverted) stitch. (Figure 9)

The center fill-in will repeat the color corresponding
to the outside rows of the pentagon.

Fig. 10

Stitch PENTAGON POINTS JUST ABOVE
THE LAST. KEEP STITCHES CLOSE TOGETHER
up the Gold Mark Lines.

At Row 3, the Pentagons' POINT PATTERNS
begin to show as they are developed by the stitch
overlaps.(Figure 10)

Continue with layers until rows fill in to 1/2
to 2/3 of the pentagon. Rows around the outside fill
in toward each adjacent center.

IF YOU CHOOSE NOT TO CUT THE THREADS
AFTER EACH ROW IS APPLIED,
THEN KEEP THEM SHORT.
When stitching a row, pull other colored threads
that are in the way toward the CENTER OF THE
PENTAGON that you are working. (Figure 11)

Fig. 11

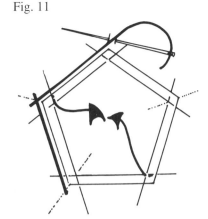

**The ball PATTERN MAY BE ENDED
after 7 ROWS ARE COMPLETED.**

Continue to stitch 1 Row for each number
until there are 7 Rows around each Pentagon.
Stitch the FINAL ROW of GOLD around all
— 1 through 6 North and 1 through 6 South.
(Figure 12)

Fig. 12

Complete the Pentagon Centers:
Stitch 5 Rows of the Same Color as the
Outside Pentagon in each Pentagon Center.
Stitch 1 Row of Gold around each of the 12 Centers.

END with
GOLD OUTLINES

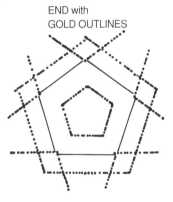

Fig. 13

PENTAGON POINTS
TOUCH

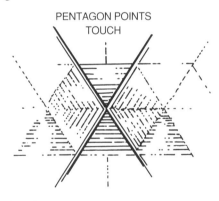

Fig. 14

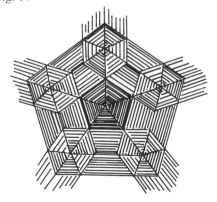

FOR AN ALL-COVERED BALL,
Continue the number pattern until 12 Rows
are completed (2 1/2 inch ball) or until all
Pentagon Points touch at their Center Mark Lines.
The CENTER SPACES will be filled in with color
rows the same as the outside pentagon.
(Figure 13)

Fill in the Center Spaces to cover the thread wrap
— about 7 Rows of the Outside Pentagon Color.
(Figure 14)

For the Final FILL-IN Row, push back the
surrounding pentagon rows. Take stitches of
final fill-in rows right up to the surrounding threads.
These will lock in place the surrounding threads.

The ball is complete.